Archaeological and Historic Pottery Production Sites

Guidelines for Best Practice

Summary

This document provides practical guidance on how to investigate sites where pottery production has taken place. It describes how to anticipate and locate pottery production sites and the types of evidence that may be found. This document also provides advice on the available methods and strategies for examining, recording and sampling features and finds of various types at each stage of the work. The different techniques for establishing the date of pottery production, and for characterising the products of a site, are given particular emphasis.

This document was compiled by Harriet White, Sarah Paynter and Duncan Brown with contributions by Joanne Best, Chris Cumberpatch, David Dawson, Peter Ellis, Jane Evans, Laurence Jones, Oliver Kent, Gareth Perry, The Prince's Regeneration Trust, Ian Roberts, Kerry Tyler and Ann Woodward. It is one of four Historic England publications concerning industrial processes in the past, the other three being:

- *Science for Historic Industries: Guidelines for the Investigation of 17th- to 19th-Century Industries*

- *Archaeological Evidence for Glassworking: Guidelines for Best Practice*

- *Archaeometallurgy: Guidelines for Best Practice.*

First published by Historic England October 2015.
All images © Historic England unless otherwise stated.

www.historicengland.org.uk/advice/technical-advice/archaeological-science/

Front cover images: clockwise from top left
Reconstruction of a 17th-century kiln from Potters Lane, Barnstaple, North Devon
© David Dawson, Oliver Kent and the Bickley Ceramics Project
Thin section from an Anglo-Saxon cremation urn
© Gareth Perry

A 14th-century kiln shown during excavation at the Teardrop site, Woolwich, London
© John Cotter and Oxford Archaeology
View of the kiln at Price, Powell and Co., Bristol, c 1940
© Bristol Museums, Galleries and Archives

Contents

Introduction 1

What these guidelines cover 1
How to use these guidelines 2
Key points 2

1 Investigating a Pottery Production Site 3

1.1 Project planning 3
1.2 Fieldwork 7
CS1 Scientific dating methods applied to pottery production sites 9
CS2 Severn Valley ware production at Newland Hopfields, Worcestershire 16
1.3 Post-excavation analysis 20
CS3 Interpreting pottery production technologies from thin sections 21
CS4 Chemical analysis of pottery 26
1.4 Archive 29
1.5 Preservation of pottery production sites .. 30
CS5 Middleport Pottery 31

2 Evidence of Pottery Production 34

2.1 Pottery kilns 34
2.2 Kiln furniture 40
2.3 Pottery wasters 40
2.4 Fuel waste 41
2.5 Buildings and related features 41
2.6 Raw material extraction, storage and processing 44
2.7 Equipment and tools 44

3 Background Information on Pottery Production in England 47

3.1 Raw materials 47
3.2 Manufacture 47
3.3 Decoration 49
3.4 Firing 51

4 Where to Get Advice 52

4.1 Further reading 52
4.2 Specialist advice 52
4.3 Organisations 52
4.4 Datasets 53
4.5 Museums, collections and resources 53
4.6 Contact Historic England 54

5 Glossary 55

6 References 58

Acknowledgements 63

Introduction

These guidelines promote good practice for investigating the remains of archaeological and historic pottery production sites. They are intended for all those advising on, planning or undertaking such work, whether setting a brief for the archaeological investigation of a known pottery production site, responding to an unexpected discovery during fieldwork or evaluating the significance of extant structures. This includes archaeologists advising local planning authorities and/or preparing briefs, project managers writing schemes of investigation or project designs, and all those working on such sites, whether development- or research-led.

What these guidelines cover

The study of pottery is an integral and well-established aspect of archaeological research, but approaches to ceramic production sites are less consistent; these guidelines aim to address this issue. Pottery production sites provide rare opportunities for developing a better understanding of the past, with widespread implications well beyond the production site itself. Three key themes will be covered:

Date and duration
There are numerous scientific dating techniques that can be applied to kilns, pottery and deposits or residues associated with these, which can be used to refine ceramic chronologies.

Technology, scale and organisation
Pottery production sites can provide detailed information on how potters worked, including the scale, spatial organisation and chronological variation of production as well as the full range of techniques, processes, equipment, structures and materials used. Wasters often exhibit a broader range of variation than that known from consumption sites.

Exchange and distribution networks
If pottery from production sites is fully characterised, making appropriate use of scientific analysis, it can be more easily matched to pottery from other assemblages, improving chronologies and providing information on pottery distribution and exchange. Even when archaeological evidence for pottery production is scarce, for example in the prehistoric period, scientific analysis of pottery can still provide information on where production may have taken place by identifying probable sources of the raw material.

This guidance covers pottery production sites, as well as features and finds relating to pottery production, from about 6,000 years ago through to the recent past in England. For the most part the focus is on sites producing vessels, rather than bricks, tiles (Pearson 2011), sanitary wares or briquetage, but much of the practical advice, for example on scientific dating, sampling and post-excavation analysis, may still apply.

Synopses of the current state of knowledge for archaeological ceramics, and the information that can be obtained by their study, are provided elsewhere (see **section 4**). These guidelines therefore provide only a brief overview and recommend other sources for further information.

How to use these guidelines

These guidelines contain the following sections.

Investigating a pottery production site
This section provides information on planning, desk-based assessment, survey, undertaking fieldwork, scientific dating, sampling, post-excavation analysis and archiving, relevant to ceramic production sites.

Evidence of pottery production
This section describes the common finds from production sites in more detail, and gives examples from England.

Background information on pottery production in England
This section gives a broad overview of pottery production processes, including when and where the processes were adopted in England.

Where to get advice
This section lists further reading, useful organisations and websites, and contacts for advice.

Glossary

References

Key points

- When a pottery production site is expected, include a named pottery specialist on the project team and ensure his or her availability, and make provision for advice, training and supervision on site

- If a pottery production site is encountered unexpectedly, contact a pottery specialist as soon as possible for advice and to arrange a site visit

- A pottery specialist experienced in working with material from the site locality is best placed to comment on the significance of the site and associated finds

- Establish strategies for excavation, selection and any on-site processing or recording of the ceramic finds with the project team; plan and budget for post-excavation analysis and archiving (see section 1)

- Before disturbing or excavating any features associated with pottery making, contact a specialist in scientific dating techniques for advice and arrange a visit to the site (see sections 1.2.1.1 and 4)

- Ensure that the pottery produced at the site is adequately recorded in terms of fabric, form and technology, to provide comparative data for other researchers (see section 1)

The Historic England science advisors and pottery specialist groups listed in section 4 are useful first points of contact.

1 Investigating a Pottery Production Site

1.1 Project planning

Many archaeological projects are initiated as part of the planning process: the principles are laid out in the National Planning Policy Framework (https://www.gov.uk/government/publications/national-planning-policy-framework--2) (NPPF 2012) and are implemented at the level of local government. When a site is subject to archaeological investigation, a written scheme of investigation (WSI) or project design will be produced that sets out the aims of all the project stages, the methodologies applied to all aspects of data gathering and the means of dissemination and archive compilation (CIfA 2008a; 2008b; 2008c; 2008d; 2009; 2012; English Heritage 2006a). The WSI or project design should also outline the scope of specialist work and the allocation of funds for employing specialists as part of the project team, as well as provision for associated costs (eg scientific analysis). Specialists [defined by the Chartered Institute for Archaeologists (CIfA) as working at their member level (MCIfA)] provide requisite expertise in a relevant subject area, for example pottery making or archaeomagnetic dating. There is potential for review during the different project stages and, if a pottery production site is an unexpected discovery, the project design, WSI and project team should be amended accordingly.

If a pottery production site is known to be within the area of investigation, it is essential to include a pottery specialist, ideally with local expertise, on the project team from the start (CIfA 2014, para 3.1.2). The pottery specialist will play a crucial role in developing site-specific research questions, which will maximise the potential for understanding the site and its products, as well as more general aspects of technology, chronology and distribution. Table 1 lists examples of the questions that can be addressed during the various project stages, including data collection, by employing specific methodological approaches.

Pottery production sites can produce huge amounts of material, especially pottery wasters, and it is necessary to work to an agreed strategy for collecting, recording, analysing and selecting (for archive and reference) all the archaeological material. The project team will establish a selection strategy for kiln products, associated materials such as kiln furniture, fragments of kiln structure, and environmental and scientific samples (see section 1.2.2). The selection strategy should be reviewed as data collection progresses, to ensure compliance with the research aims of the project and compatibility with the collecting policy of the project archive repository; a representative of the repository should also be included on the project team. A post-excavation budget must be agreed, taking into account the scale of the task and the specialist input required.

Theme	Questions	Methods of investigation
Pottery organisation	When was pottery made at the site?	Documentary records, excavation, scientific dating, typological evidence
Pottery organisation	What is the extent and layout of the production site?	Documentary records, geophysical survey, open-area excavation
Pottery organisation	Are there features associated with clay extraction and preparation, such as clay pits, levigation systems, mixing floors or placements for blungers or mills?	Documentary records, geophysical survey, open-area excavation, sampling, analysis
Pottery organisation	Is there evidence for processing other raw materials, including glazes, pigments or tempering materials, for example features or finds associated with milling, fritting or drying?	Documentary records, open-area excavation, sampling, analysis
Pottery organisation	Where were raw materials, including fuel, tools and equipment, stored?	Documentary records, geophysical survey, open-area excavation, sampling, analysis
Pottery organisation	Is there evidence to indicate where different production processes took place, for example potting, drying, dipping and printing?	Documentary records, open-area excavation
Pottery organisation	How many and what types of kilns were in use and for how long? If more than one were they contemporaneous or did they have different functions?	Documentary records, geophysical survey, excavation, scientific dating, typological assessment of vessels
Production technologies	What types of pottery were made at the site and how were they manufactured? Were they coil-built, slab-built, turned, wheel-thrown, moulded or slip-cast? Are there any surviving tools, moulds or associated features?	Documentary records, typological assessment of vessels, investigation of surface markings, petrographic analysis, chemical analysis, assessment of related finds
Production technologies	How were the kilns constructed, how did they operate and how were they fuelled?	Documentary records, excavation, environmental analysis, chemical analysis, assessment to identify fragments of kiln structure
Production technologies	How was the pottery stacked in the kilns: were props, spacers, trivets or saggars used? Were glazed and unglazed vessels fired together?	Documentary records, assessment of associated finds to identify kiln furniture and wasters, examination of surface markings on vessels
Production technologies	Were the vessels fired once or more? How closely was the atmosphere controlled?	Documentary records, macroscopic examination of sherds and fragments of kiln structure, petrographic analysis
Production technologies	What clay sources were used and how was the clay modified, for example mixing clays, adding temper or colourants, making a slip for casting or decoration?	Documentary records, petrographic analysis, chemical analysis, geological sampling of nearby sources or storage pits
Production technologies	How were the vessels decorated? Do raw materials, tools or equipment used for decorating surfaces survive?	Documentary records, assessment of associated finds to identify tools and equipment, analysis of vessel surfaces or raw material deposits
Economic and wider contexts	What were the level, scale and longevity of production?	Documentary records, sherd quantification, scientific dating
Economic and wider contexts	How do the products from the site relate to pottery recovered from consumer sites? How was the pottery transported, distributed and used?	Documentary records, comparison of vessel forms and fabrics, and of petrographic and chemical data, topographical assessment

Table 1
Examples of research questions that can be addressed at pottery production sites, and the investigation methods that can be employed

It is important to schedule site visits as soon as the site type is identified, particularly for the collection of samples for scientific dating, to ensure that qualified specialists are available at appropriate points during the excavation (see section 1.2.2.1).

1.1.1 Contaminated land

Some of the raw materials used in pottery production are hazardous, in particular the lead compounds used for glazing and the metal compounds used as pigments and colourants. If there is evidence that lead glazes or toxic pigments were used at a site, then a risk assessment is required to establish safe working procedures. More information on land contamination is available in *Science for Historic Industries* (English Heritage 2006b, 32), and from CIfA (http://www.archaeologists.net), the Environment Agency (http://www.environment-agency.gov.uk) and DEFRA (http://www.defra.gov.uk).

1.1.2 Anticipating pottery production sites

The raw materials required for pottery production (clay, fuel, water and temper) are easily found, and therefore pottery production sites are widespread across the country (Simco 1998; 2000). Pottery production was carried out in many different contexts and settings, domestic, small- and large-scale, rural and urban, by people with varying degrees of specialist skill. There are a number of ways of establishing whether or not a pottery production site is likely to be present in a particular area.

1.1.2.1 Current knowledge

Known archaeological activity for a given area is recorded in Historic Environment Records (HERs) and Urban Archaeological Databases (UADs). HERs and UADs are collated and maintained by local authorities; contact details for local HERs can be found at the Heritage Gateway website (http://www.heritagegateway.org.uk/gateway). Regional research frameworks can be accessed through the Association of Local Government Archaeological Officers' (ALGAO) website (http://www.algao.org.uk/england/research_frameworks). A number of national and research frameworks also provide reviews specifically relating to pottery production and pottery studies (Irving 2011; Perrin 2011); topics that would benefit from further research in a given region are highlighted (see section 4). Local and county museum collections may include relevant artefacts and documentation from previous fieldwork.

1.1.2.2 Historical sources

An overview of valuable resources is given by Crossley in *Science for Historic Industries* (English Heritage 2006b, 22–5). These include Ordnance Survey maps from the mid-19th century and county maps from the late 16th century onwards, but also fire insurance and sale plans. Historical documents such as maps (Fig 1), estate accounts and legal records may indicate the presence of a production site in a locality, or identify possible pottery makers through surnames such as Crocker or Potter, although a potter-derived surname is a less reliable indicator by the later medieval period (Le Patourel 1968, 103). Place names (eg Crockerton) can also point to past potting activities in an area.

Public records, including rate books, by-laws and parliamentary records, can be supplemented with information from private archives, some of which can be searched online through the Access to Archives project (http://www.a2a.org.uk). Other business archives have been catalogued by the National Register of Archives of the Historical Manuscripts Commission. Legal records are useful for the 16th and 17th centuries.

Landscape paintings and then photographs (Fig 2) are increasingly available online through websites such as Viewfinder (http://viewfinder.HistoricEngland.org.uk) and Pastscape (http://www.pastscape.org.uk/), and can indicate the existence of a production site at a particular date. Contemporary publications, including newspapers, various lists, encyclopaedias, textbooks, images and film, can provide records of industrial processes, factory tours or descriptions and illustrations of premises (Fig 3); however, these may require expert interpretation.

Figures 1 and 2

1. A 19th-century map showing the layout of Bristol Temple Back pottery, Bristol, with two biscuit and two glost kilns, a hardening kiln and an enamel kiln, and specified areas for plate-making, dipping and placing, drying, printing, throwing and milling raw materials.
© Bristol Museums, Galleries and Archives

2. Postcard of 'The Olde Pottery, Donyatt', Somerset, c 1900, from the Anning Collection.
© Somerset Heritage Service

Figure 3
A 19th-century illustration of wares being placed in protective saggars before loading into bottle kilns (from Cuddon 1827).

1.2 Fieldwork

1.2.1 Non-intrusive investigation methods

Geophysical survey techniques can reveal evidence of pottery production through the identification of kilns and waster dumps as characteristic anomalies (English Heritage 2008a). With open sites, a magnetometer survey is particularly useful in areas of high temperature industrial activity, as it can detect thermoremanently magnetised features such as kilns. Pits, ditches, gullies, postholes (>0.5m diameter) and hearths can also be plotted, which will help determine the extent of a site. Such results can be used to position excavation areas, as can site topography, where mounds may indicate waste tips.

Fieldwalking and surface collection, especially of pottery wasters and other production waste, will contribute to the identification of a pottery production site and inform subsequent strategies for intrusive investigation, characterisation and preservation.

1.2.2 Intrusive fieldwork

Intrusive fieldwork, whether as part of a field evaluation or archaeological excavation, may reveal kilns and waste dumps, which are often the clearest indicators of pottery production. A pottery production site comprises more than kilns and wasters, however; there are likely to be many associated features and structures that warrant investigation, such as extraction or levigation pits, stores or workshops, potentially with tools, working floors and raw material deposits, and settlement activity (see section 2). Where possible, excavation areas should be positioned based on the results of advance survey and target the full range of features and structures associated with the production site, not just the kilns; often the maximum potential of pottery production sites is only realised during open-area excavation (Best et al 2013), allowing more ephemeral features to be identified and revealing how potters organised and continually adapted their working area (Moorhouse 1981). For example, it is common for Roman kilns to be constructed within ditched enclosures, which may also contain waste from phases of activity that are otherwise poorly represented.

It is essential to include a pottery specialist on the project team from the outset if the nature of the site is known, and at the earliest opportunity if it becomes apparent at a later stage. The pottery specialist can provide supervision and training for site staff to ensure that features and finds from pottery production are recognised and interpreted appropriately. Advice from a specialist will lead to increased awareness of the processes and associated structures that leave little trace archaeologically and are easily missed, for example clamp kilns, clay preparation areas or pottery drying racks (see section 2). Similarly, a specialist is more likely to recognise finds with the potential to improve understanding of the production process, for example derive information on how the kiln was constructed, loaded and operated, from fragmentary kiln remains, glaze marks on kiln furniture or makers' marks on pottery. An experienced specialist is able to help with the identification of more unusual types of artefacts, for example potters' tools or equipment and kiln furniture (see section 2.2), which can take a diverse range of forms depending on the period and type of ware.

Finally a specialist can advise on site formation and deposition processes; wasters are frequently redeposited in kilns, or occasionally used in kiln construction or as a type of kiln furniture, and in these contexts are easily misidentified as the final load of that kiln.

Possible kilns and other discrete features should be excavated in their entirety, to understand better how they were constructed and functioned, to find evidence of repair or modification, to understand how they were demolished or backfilled and to obtain material for scientific dating or environmental sampling, commonly from stoke pits (see case study 1). Excavation by quadrants or segments enables a complete longitudinal section and transverse sections to be recorded for the various elements of the kiln or firing area. The remains of post-medieval and later kilns are likely to include complex flue systems below ground (Barker and Goodwin 2006); accurate recording of these features is essential for establishing how the kiln functioned. The contents of the kiln or firing area, including wasters, fuel, firing furniture, fired clay and fragmentary kiln structure, should be retained, washed, processed and recorded (see section 1.3). Different phases of dumping may be apparent in large waste tips or the backfill of kilns, for example as in the 17th-century Tin-glazed kiln at Southwark Cathedral, London (Divers and Jarrett 2008). In such cases, the contents of each phase should be recovered separately as they can provide information on the chronological development of the site and its products. Stratified deposits may also have potential for modelling to refine scientific dates (see section 1.2.2.1).

Case study 1: scientific dating methods applied to pottery production sites

Tinney's Lane, Sherborne, Dorset, from Best and Woodward (2012) and Best et al (2013)

Excavations at Tinney's Lane found evidence of Late Bronze Age pottery production, including areas of heat-affected clay where open firings may have taken place, and nearby features that were backfilled with waste from pottery production, including a high proportion of burnt sherds and perforated fired clay objects (the latter are potentially a type of firing furniture). The assemblage of plainware pottery from Tinney's Lane is one of the largest ever recovered, comprising nearly 14,000 sherds (Fig CS1: A).

Twenty-four samples of short-lived charcoal from the site were submitted for radiocarbon dating; these were from the burnt features probably used for open firings and also from associated pits containing single dumps of waste such as burnt sherds, ashy deposits and fired clay. The probable dates of pottery production were estimated by using a model (Fig CS1: A) that combined the radiocarbon dates with archaeological information, providing an estimate for the start of ceramic production at Tinney's Lane of *1200–1050 cal BC (95% probability; start_pottery_production*; Fig CS1: A) and probably *1150–1070 cal BC (68% probability)*, and for the end of production of *1100–950 cal BC (95% probability; end_pottery_production*; Fig CS1: A) and probably *1050–980 cal BC (68% probability)*. The date of pottery production at Tinney's Lane and the morphological characteristics of the assemblage suggest, along with those from Kemerton, Worcestershire, and Eynsham Abbey, Oxfordshire, a newly recognised ceramic subphase in the earliest part of the Late Bronze Age.

Simpson's Malt, Pontefract, West Yorkshire, from Cumberpatch et al (2013), Greenwood et al (2010) and Roberts and Cumberpatch (2009)

A well-preserved pottery kiln (Fig CS1: B) and its surrounds were excavated at Simpson's Malt by Archaeological Services WYAS in 2008 in advance of a housing development. (The full report is available from http://archaeologydataservice.ac.uk/archives/view/simpson_eh_2012). It was difficult to relate the surrounding features to the kiln but it was established that the output was Stamford ware-type pottery, a significant discovery as previously this was assumed to have been manufactured only in Stamford itself (Fig CS1: C). The Pontefract version was in two fabrics, one of which was visually identical to the Stamford products and could often be identified by means of a distinctive wheel-stamp motif. The represented vessel types fell late in the Stamford ware sequence and were found in deposits with local style gritty ware, which is generally accepted as post-Conquest (Cumberpatch et al 2013; Roberts and Cumberpatch 2009).

Single fragments of short-lived charcoal from the floor and stoke pit of the kiln provided a number of samples for radiocarbon dating. Chronological modelling of the radiocarbon dates (Fig CS1: D) provided an estimate for the last firing of cal AD 990–1050 (95% probability; kiln firing; Fig CS1: D), probably cal AD 1000–1040 (68% probability). Although the undisturbed conditions of the kiln were ideal for archaeomagnetic dating, the measurements were atypical and there was a discrepancy between the archaeomagnetic and radiocarbon dating results (Greenwood et al 2010).

The limited distribution of the Simpson's Malt products suggests that production was probably short-lived and, based upon the scientific dating (which indicates the last firing of the excavated kiln and not the date range of production at Simpson's Malt), took place only shortly before the Norman Conquest. Nonetheless the estimated date for the last firing of this kiln is significantly earlier than the late 11th- to 12th-century date anticipated on typological grounds and from the archaeological associations at a number of consumption sites (Cumberpatch et al 2013; Greenwood et al 2010). The implications are potentially far reaching for our understanding of the economy and society in the immediate area and could give rise to a re-evaluation of several aspects of the production and use of pre- and post-Conquest pottery in the region. This would involve revisiting the pottery archives for late Saxon and early medieval sites in Yorkshire, so also demonstrates the importance of retaining adequate pottery archives for future study.

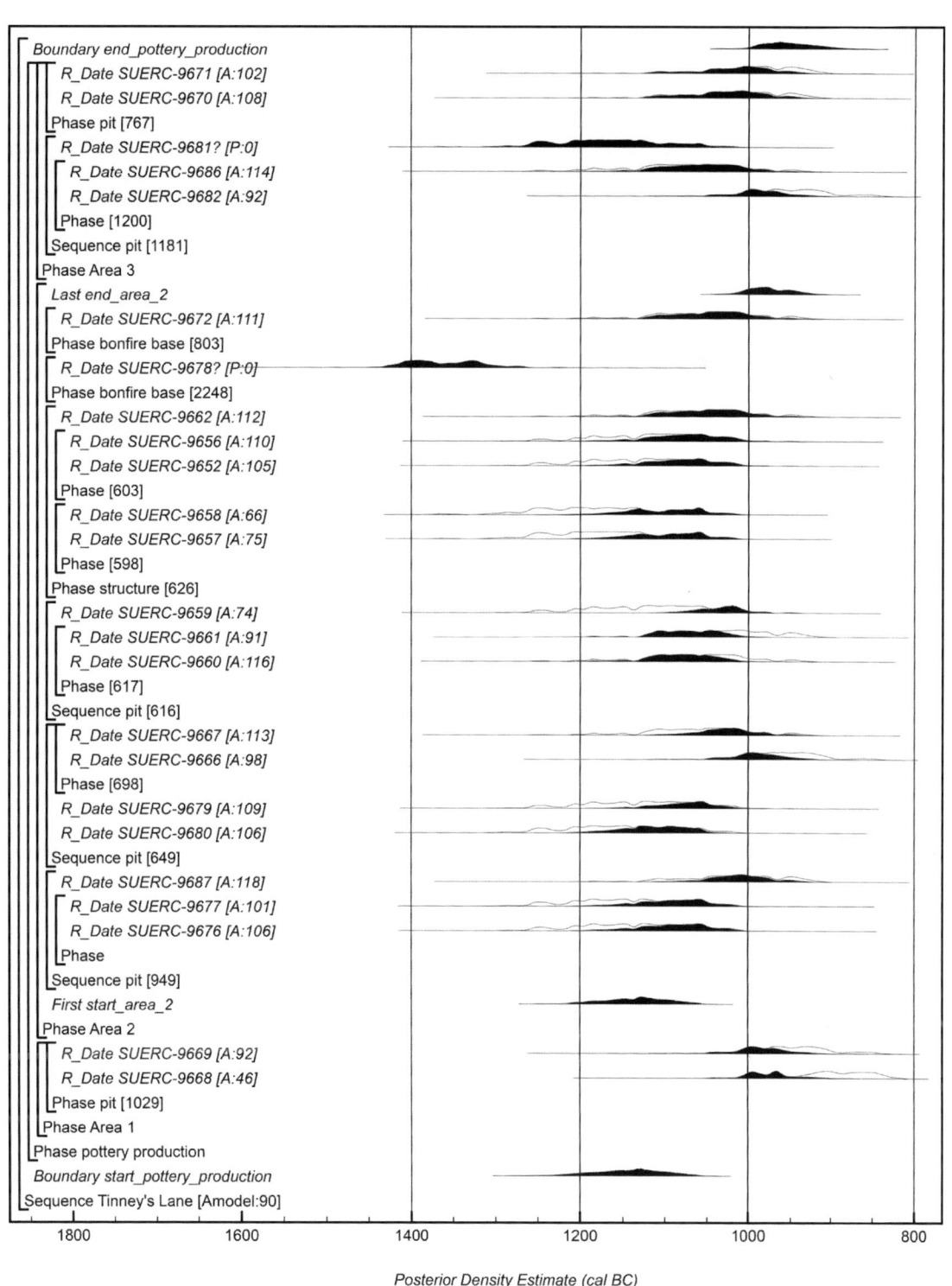

Figure CS1: A

A. Probability distributions of dates from Tinney's Lane, Sherborne, Dorset. Each distribution represents the relative probability that an event occurs at a particular time. For each radiocarbon date, two distributions have been plotted: one in outline, which is the result of simple radiocarbon calibration, and a solid one based on the chronological model used. The other distributions correspond to aspects of the model. For example, the distribution 'start_pottery_production' is the estimate for the beginning of pottery manufacture. The large square brackets down the left-hand side of the diagram and the OxCal keywords define the overall model exactly.
© Peter Marshall

Figure CS1: B
Pottery kiln remains at Simpson's Malt, Pontefract, West Yorkshire; the date of the last firing was estimated using Bayesian modelling of radiocarbon dates (Fig CS1: D).
© Ian Roberts

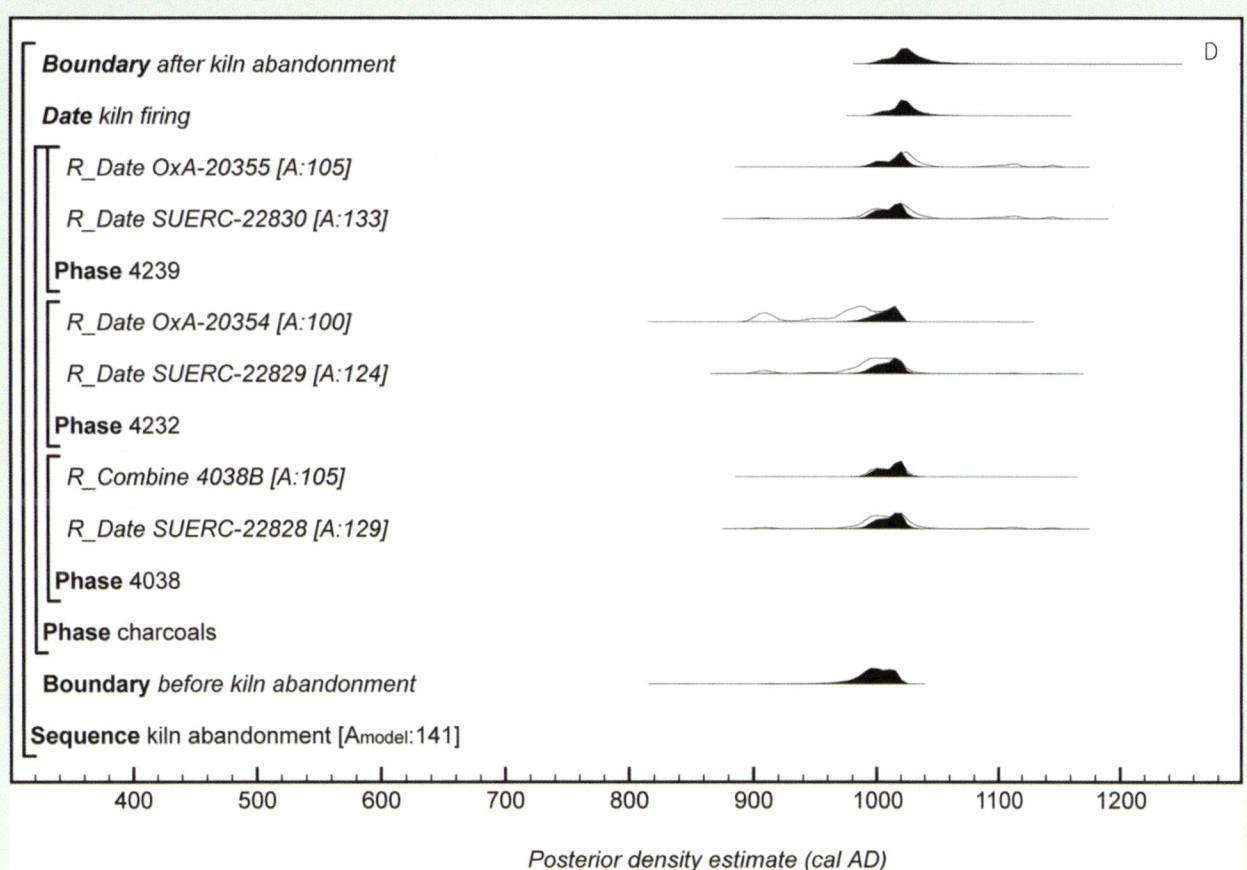

Figure CS1: C and D
C. Stamford-type ware from Simpson's Malt, Pontefract, West Yorkshire, dating to the 11th century AD.
© Ian Roberts
D. Chronological model of the Simpson's Malt, Pontefract, West Yorkshire, radiocarbon results; distributions in outline are from a simple calibration of radiocarbon results, the solid distributions are posterior density estimates of the dates of samples and events.
© John Meadows

It is standard for spreads, dumps or pits that can be directly related to production to be fully excavated; this includes features in the vicinity of the kilns themselves but also those containing a large proportion of wasters or kiln furniture and superstructure, which are thereby linked to production. This is particularly important for prehistoric and early medieval sites, where firing areas are generally more difficult to recognise and may contain very little diagnostic material; the presence of firing furniture, fired clay and wasters in adjacent pits and ditches may be essential for identifying the firing area or kiln itself (Best *et al* 2013*)*. Storage pits, levigation pits and clay extraction pits are likely to require full excavation to establish their purpose and to obtain samples of their contents for identification and study. Extended features, such as ditches, are more likely to be investigated by excavating slots representing at least 10 per cent of the feature, for example, but this should be reassessed if the feature or its fill provides evidence of particular note.

Many Roman, medieval and later potteries operated on a substantial scale, perhaps using multiple kilns for some duration, occasionally resulting in large amounts of waste (eg Moorhouse and Roberts 1992; Seeley and Drummond-Murray 2005). If the production waste on a site potentially comprises tens of thousands of sherds, a selection strategy should be considered; if selection is required, then it will also be necessary for an element of washing, sorting and recording of finds to take place on site. The most appropriate approach will vary on a site to site basis so it is essential that a pottery specialist is involved in developing this strategy (see section 1.2.2.2).

1.2.2.1 Dating the period of production

Providing robust chronologies for pottery production sites, such as the last firing of a kiln(s), is important to determine the currency of ceramic types (see case study 1). It is therefore essential that samples and measurements for the scientific dating of kiln structures are collected in the field. As this specialised task can only be carried out by qualified personnel, this requirement needs to be included in the project planning stage, with a specialist named in the documentation. The availability of the specialist should be confirmed as soon as the site type is identified, to ensure that he or she is able to visit the site when kiln features and associated deposits are uncovered. The Historic England science advisors should be the first point of contact for further advice on scientific dating; they can provide lists of laboratories and specialists on request (see section 4.6). Further information is also available in the relevant English Heritage guidance documents on scientific dating (Duller 2008; English Heritage 2006c). This section reviews the main dating techniques relevant to pottery production sites; others may become available in future, for example rehydroxylation (RHX) dating (Wilson *et al* 2012*)*.

Archaeomagnetic dating

Directional archaeomagnetic dating is the most commonly used archaeomagnetic technique in the UK. Dating is most precise using this method for the post-medieval period to the present, but there is also potential for good precision in earlier periods (English Heritage 2006b; 2006c). Kiln remains are ideally suited to archaeomagnetic dating because the materials used in their construction (brick, tile, clay or stone) commonly contain magnetic minerals, and during their use they are heated to temperatures in excess of those required to fix a remanent magnetism. The event dated will be the final firing of the kiln, providing it was high enough to reset the remanent magnetism of previous firings.

The method relies upon the direction of the Earth's magnetic field varying with time. The remanent magnetism of the feature is determined and compared with an archaeomagnetic calibration curve to determine its best-fit date range. If kiln remains are highly fired and structurally intact, with no signs of disturbance or movement, for example as a result of tree roots, slumping or cracking, then the kiln is likely to be suitable for archaeomagnetic dating.

Radiocarbon dating

Charcoal is one of the most commonly used materials for radiocarbon dating, and is often associated with pottery kilns because wood was one of the primary fuels used. The method dates the last time an organism exchanged carbon with the biosphere; in the case of charcoal, the event dated is the growth of the tree-ring(s) sampled (Bowman 1990). For long-lived species, for example oak, there can be a large (potentially hundreds of years) age-at-death offset, between the age of a sample and the event of interest. Therefore short-lived material (twigs or short-lived tree species) or the outer rings (sapwood) of long-lived species should be selected for dating in order to provide an indication of when the kiln was used. Samples should be taken from kiln stoking pits, ash pits or firing chambers and processed as for environmental remains (English Heritage 2011a). A charcoal specialist can then identify and select single fragments of material for radiocarbon dating.

Luminescence dating

Luminescence dating can be used to date fired structures or objects (Duller 2008), including bricks, terracotta and ceramics. The technique measures the energy that has become trapped in minerals in the clay since the material was last fired or exposed to light, and so dates the last firing of the material dated. Precision is usually 5–10 per cent of the age of the object (eg ±5–10 years for an object that is 100 years old, but ±100–200 years for an object that is 2000 years old). If dating a kiln, the specialist should be contacted during fieldwork so that *in situ* radiation measurements can be made; these will improve the precision of the quoted age. Standing structures can also be sampled. Where possible, pottery sherds should be more than 10mm thick and more than 30mm across, taken from at least 0.3m below the current ground surface, and accompanied by a soil sample that can be used for measurement of water content and elemental concentrations / dose-rate of the deposit. Other ceramics, such as those from museum stores, can also be dated but precision will be lower.

Bayesian chronological modelling

For a single sample, calibration of the radiocarbon age (or of the weighted mean if there is more than one determination on the sample) is sufficient to convert the radiocarbon measurement to the calendar timescale. For a group of radiocarbon ages from samples that are in some way related, however, a more sophisticated statistical approach is required. Bayesian chronological modelling provides an explicit, probabilistic method for combining different sorts of evidence to estimate the dates of events that happened in the past and for quantifying the uncertainties of these estimates. Rigour in sample selection, and the need for explicit consideration of archaeological information in interpretation, means that guidance should be sought at an early stage (see case study 1 and section 4).

1.2.2.2 Finds selection for recording, post-excavation study and archiving

This is a complex issue, particularly on large-scale sites where massive waste tips can be encountered. It is not possible to prescribe a general method that is equally applicable to all sites because each one is different. A project team will have to decide what is most appropriate for the site in question; the team should include all interested parties, including the pottery specialist, the project executive (usually the archaeologist who set the brief), the project manager (representing the organisation that developed the WSI or project design) and the curator of the repository that will receive the project archive. These representatives should also be invited to visit the site during fieldwork, particularly when establishing or modifying the selection strategy. Project-specific research questions should drive the selection strategy and any decision on what material to retain; some examples of the different approaches that have been adopted on large-scale sites are described in this section. Further information on selection can be found in the guidance produced by the Archaeological Archives Forum (Brown 2011).

Developing a strategy for selection

It is usually the contents of waster dumps (and also unstratified material) that is subject to selection (see section 1.2.2 for general approaches to excavation). Ceramic waste is likely to be the most commonly encountered material, including pottery fragments and kiln furniture, such as saggars and props, separators or lumps of clay that were used in stacking the kiln. It is not uncommon for a production site to produce many thousands of sherds, particularly if there are multiple kilns in the excavated area, and there may be tens of tonnes of waste at post-medieval and later sites (Fig 4). In such cases, early consideration of selection strategies, for recording, for study and for archive, is essential. The input of the pottery specialist is critical in deciding the selection strategy, and in advising, training and supervising staff while they are working with the pottery on site.

The size of the assemblage is only one consideration when deciding whether to select material; the significance of the site is dependent on many factors, including the date, regional context, level of preservation and type of kiln products. Examples of recently excavated production sites with large quantities of waste, where all of the excavated material was recovered, include the 11th-century Simpson's Malt, Pontefract, West Yorkshire, and Late Bronze Age Tinney's Lane, Sherborne, Dorset (see case study 1); the assemblages at each comprised approximately 13,000 sherds. Substantial assemblages of around 6,000 sherds were retained from the Roman site at Newland Hopfields, Worcestershire (see case study 2) and around 4,000 from the six Roman kilns at the Moorfield Road site, Duxford, Cambridgeshire (Pre-Construct Archaeology Ltd 2014). A selection strategy was employed for the multiple kilns at the medieval Teardrop site, Woolwich, London (Cotter 2008), where all of the wasters from the kilns were retained but material was selected from waster tips, leading to the retention of tens of thousands of sherds. The Roman production site at Walbrook, London, produced in excess of 30,000 sherds; this included material from the kilns and other features (pits and dumps) in the main production area and selected material from features elsewhere (Seeley and Drummond-Murray 2005). Selection was also employed at the 19th-century pottery production site at Grimshaw, Lancashire, resulting in around 5,000 sherds being processed (Oxford Archaeology North 2012).

Figure 4
Medieval pottery wasters from one of the kilns at the Teardrop site, Woolwich, London.
© John Cotter and Oxford Archaeology

Case study 2: Severn Valley ware production at Newland Hopfields, Worcestershire

From Evans et al (2000)

Newland Hopfields and the surrounding area was known to be a possible pottery production site because of surface scatters of pottery, waster dumps and kiln remains found there in the past. A planned development therefore included provision for archaeological investigation with a pottery specialist involved from the earliest stages. Areas of interest were identified using geophysical survey, field walking and trial trenching.

The badly truncated remains of a single-flue Romano-British kiln were identified in one area, and others had probably been destroyed by ploughing. The excavation encompassed the area surrounding the surviving kiln and revealed possible levigation ditches and cobbled surfaces, probably for processing clay, a well, a group of keyhole-shaped hearths, polishing stones and postholes. These features and objects were probably associated with pottery production, for example the postholes may be indicative of drying racks. There was little pottery within the kiln itself but large quantities in the surrounding ditches and pits, with kiln debris, charcoal and slag waste.

Almost a third of the material identified as kiln debris had imprints of vegetation, showing turves were used in the kiln superstructure. Other pieces had imprints of sticks or wattles and there were also some preformed blocks. A few pottery wasters were fused to kiln fragments, and may have been used to reinforce the structure. Environmental samples provided charcoal from which the species used as fuel were identified, but no evidence of coppicing was found.

All of the pottery from the excavated features was examined, comprising 896kg. The sherd count and mass were recorded by context to produce a broad quantification. The next stage of detailed recording included base estimated vessel equivalents (EVE), rim EVE, examination with a low-power microscope, and noting the sherd hardness. For the Severn Valley ware, only feature sherds were recorded in detail, such as rims, bases, handles, decorated body sherds and other diagnostic form sherds, but all of the sherds were recorded for other types of ware as these were far fewer. As with many kiln assemblages, there was a greater range of fabric variation than is typical of consumption sites, and so a site-specific fabric series was developed. Once recording was complete, petrological and chemical analyses were used to check the distinctiveness of these fabric types, which were then cross-referenced with the existing county fabric type series.

The kiln itself contained very little pottery but the probable products were determined by comparing the proportions of different ware in features near the kiln, and also in fills containing a large proportion of kiln furniture and debris, which all had a similar composition. Most of the pottery was wheel-made Severn Valley ware but some Malvernian ware, largely handmade, was also present. The Malvernian ware was coarsely tempered and could be identified with certainty using petrography because it contained coarse inclusions of distinctive minerals (Peacock 1968); this was not the case for Severn Valley fabrics, so these were further characterised using neutron activation analysis (NAA).

During recording, different types of temper were found in the Severn Valley wares, including charcoal-tempered fabrics, which were little known before. These tempers varied chronologically and also with the variant being made. By careful examination of the waster sherds it was possible to work out which variations were intentional and which accidental, for example the reduction of some Severn Valley fabrics appeared to be unintentional. Material was then selected for illustration

Figure CS2: A
Romano-British pottery wasters from Newland Hopfields, Worcestershire.
© Jane Evans

(CS2 continued)
as a form type series. The type series and information on fabric variability are particularly useful for specialists classifying the same pottery at consumption sites. Characteristics, such as sherd abrasion and weight, were used to determine how much the pottery dumps had been disturbed before the site was levelled.

In common with many kiln sites, there was little artefactual evidence that could be used to refine the site dating except for the pottery, and the established date ranges for Severn Valley ware forms are broad, spanning a century or more in many cases. Unfortunately no independent dates were obtained for the pottery production; there is potential to improve the chronology for this ware by dating future kiln sites using archaeomagnetic or radiocarbon dating (Fig CS2: A).

If selection of waste tips is warranted, it is important first to establish the nature of the contents (see **case study 2**). For example, how deep is the tip, are there phases of dumping, are kiln furniture or kiln superstructure present, are there different fabrics, forms and styles of decoration, are there makers' marks or pencil marks, biscuit-fired or glazed pottery, and are the diagnostic or feature sherds a small, or large, proportion of the assemblage? This assessment requires the participation of, close supervision by and guidance of the pottery specialist, and should be undertaken for material from different parts of the tip to establish whether it is fairly uniform throughout or highly variable. It is likely that the material will require cursory washing to identify certain features; if this is undertaken using a hose or other aggressive method, then fragile material, including biscuit-fired, glazed or lightly fired pottery, should be separated out by hand first to avoid damage. Once the nature of the tip has been established, a selection strategy can be decided.

If it is agreed that some material can be discarded, it is important to document the selection strategy and also to record the amount and type of material that has not been retained. A record should be included in the site archive of where and how the non-retained material was disposed of.

Material selected for study

If selection of waste tips or unstratified material takes place, it should be under the close supervision of the pottery specialist. Diagnostic vessel components, such as rims, bases, handles, spouts, distinctive body sherds or decorative elements, are often selected preferentially because these tend to have more potential for quantification and for establishing vessel types, sizes, forms and decoration, than fragmentary and featureless body sherds. However, the material selected should represent every colour and texture of fabric present, together with all types of decoration and surface treatment. The selection should also include material from all stages of production, such as biscuit-fired ware, sherds with pencil marks or other makers' marks, painted sherds, sherds with unfired applied glaze, and glost-fired sherds (Fig 5). A similar strategy is required for kiln furniture and pieces of kiln structure, ensuring that all types are represented; the advice of a fired clay specialist may be beneficial for the latter. Examples of the different types of waster, such as blistered, melted or warped pieces, should also be represented in the sample, particularly where these are adhered to, or *in situ* with, the relevant kiln furniture or saggars. Complete or largely intact vessels should be retained. If there are depositional patterns to the waste dump, indicating the production sequence, the scale and failure rate of each stage, or changes in fabric, form or decoration over time, then material needs to be taken from each dumping episode and recorded as from different contexts.

In addition to the selected material, bulk samples can be useful as an indication of the original composition of the tip. However, bulk samples may only contain a very small proportion of the diagnostic sherds that are needed to answer key questions about the site, and so bulk sampling is not recommended in place of selection. For example, a waste tip may comprise largely biscuit-fired wasters, with only a very small proportion of decorated sherds; therefore even a large bulk sample may not recover enough decorated sherds to characterise the kiln products adequately.

Figures 5 and 6
5. Biscuit sherds of a 17th-century *sgraffito*-decorated plate from Potters Lane, Barnstaple, North Devon. Slipwares are unusual in being biscuit-fired then glaze-fired instead of the more normal, single, raw-glaze firing.
© The Museum of Barnstaple and North Devon
6. Bricks and tiles used in the construction of the 17th-century kiln 2 at site 13 of the Donyatt potteries, Somerset.
© David Dawson and Chard Museum

The amounts of material kept overall should be judged statistically sufficient for post-excavation analyses and study, for all contexts, phases and material types (Fig 6); this depends on how much similar material has been retained from other contexts on site, such as the kiln (see **case study 2**). If a selection strategy must be employed nonetheless, the sample retained for study is typically a substantial proportion of the whole, such as a third. Approaches to recording the material are discussed in **section 1.3** and **case study 2**, and to archiving in **section 1.4**.

1.2.2.3 Raw materials

Features used for storing or processing raw materials may be found at pottery production sites, such as levigation tanks or deposits of glazing mixtures. Scientific analysis of these deposits will enable the material to be identified. Suitable precautions should be taken if lead glaze or pigments could have been used at the site (see **section 1.1.1**).

Some analytical equipment is now available, such as the portable X-ray fluorescence device (p-XRF), that can be used on site by a specialist with appropriate expertise; however, most analysis will still be undertaken in a laboratory and this requires samples to be taken (English Heritage 2006b). Most analytical techniques can, if necessary, make use of small samples of a few grams or less, but the larger the sample the more representative it will be of the bulk deposit. Samples of 1kg or more can also be used for experimental work and firing tests. The type and number of samples required will depend on the nature of the find; for example, if there are differences apparent within the deposit, such as surface alteration or deposition layers, then a monolith tin or core can be used.

1.2.2.4 Environmental evidence

A range of environmental evidence may be associated with a ceramic production site. Charred fuel sometimes survives, and should be sampled and processed (English Heritage 2011a) so that the fuel type can be identified together with possible evidence for woodland management; these samples can also be used for radiocarbon dating. Other evidence, such as molluscan assemblages and charred plants, provide further information on the past environment and sometimes the raw material sources as well; for example, the presence of aquatic and marshland species at the Late Bronze Age pottery production site at Tinney's Lane, Sherborne, Dorset, showed that materials such as fresh water, reeds and clay were gathered from the nearby riverside (Best *et al* 2013).

Off-site sampling should also be considered during project planning, with specialists named in the project documentation. Organic material survives well in waterlogged conditions, so sufficiently thick sediments in nearby wetland environments may preserve evidence of changes to the surroundings as a result of industrial activity. Core samples can be examined for pollen and charred particles, from which it may be possible to build up a picture of the environmental impact of nearby pottery production over time, particularly in later periods. Evidence of heavy metal pollution from the use of glazes or pigments may be apparent in sediments from nearby rivers.

1.2.2.5 Lifting, processing and short-term storage of finds

Pottery is likely to be the most common find at a production site but other objects, such as kiln furniture, tools and equipment, may also be recovered, along with associated deposits such as raw materials, fuel waste and working surfaces. Pottery-making tools may be of metal, bone, wood or stone, and should be handled, treated and packed according to current best practice and national standards, with the advice of a conservator as appropriate (Brown 2011; English Heritage 2008b; Watkinson and Neal 2001).

Highly fired ceramics, such as those produced in updraught kilns, tend to be very robust, but open-fired ceramics, or ceramics with shell or calcite inclusions, can become friable and fragile in certain burial conditions and require careful handling. Surface decoration on ceramics is more vulnerable; some conditions can cause applied surfaces, such as glazes, slips and pigments, to delaminate from the surface, and so rigorous washing should be avoided. At kiln sites there may also be wasters from different stages of the production process with, for example, glazes or pigments that have been applied but not fired and are therefore fragile. Low-fired wares are also vulnerable, including prehistoric pottery, Roman greywares, tin-glazed earthenware and some medieval sandy wares. Masking tape, parcel tape and other adhesive tapes are not suitable for reconstructing pottery; instead, individual vessels and joining sherds should be bagged together.

It is important that the condition of ceramics is assessed upon excavation by a finds specialist or conservator, and the strategy for finds processing adapted if necessary. It may be necessary to lift fragile ceramics or complete vessels within the surrounding matrix of earth for subsequent excavation in a laboratory. All ceramics should be fully dried out prior to packing in bags and boxes. Complete ceramic vessels or large fragments should be supported by pads of acid-free tissue paper and stored in robust boxes, preferably cardboard.

1.3 Post-excavation analysis

A variety of techniques may be applied to answer questions about pottery production at a site, such as the dates of production, the character of the products, how they were made and their development through time, the scale and levels of organisation of the production site and the extent of distribution of the products. Although the following section focuses largely on pottery, the associated firing furniture, kiln fragments and raw materials also require post-excavation study and the same analytical techniques can be applied in many cases.

If samples for scientific dating have not been collected during excavation, then it is very difficult to provide absolute dates for the period of production (see **section 1.2.2.1**). Relative dates can be achieved by typological analysis of pottery types and analysis of the stratigraphic sequence, using comparative finds from other sites, such as domestic contexts in towns.

1.3.1 Recording the pottery

Pottery is characterised and sorted according to fabric type, overall vessel form, the shape of component parts, rim diameter and vessel size, technology (such as method of manufacture) and types of surface treatment, decorative techniques and motifs. Analysis and recording of all of these should be carried out by an experienced and qualified ceramic specialist on washed material (see **case study 2**). Once sorted, the quantity of different types present is also recorded, usually by mass (in grams), sherd count and vessel number (or equivalent) (Orton and Hughes, 2013). On production sites, in theory, accurate vessel quantities are achievable and the recording process should aim to provide as close an understanding as possible of vessel output.

1.3.1.1 Fabric

The techniques of fabric characterisation, especially using hand specimens, are covered elsewhere (Orton and Hughes 2013). In brief, the description is generally based on an examination using a hand lens or low magnification microscope, and illustrated by photographs of a fresh break. The fabric description provides information on the qualities of the clay, the use of temper and the colours produced, which will all shed light on the way the potters worked and what they aimed to make. The fabrics identified at a site should be described with reference to the local or regional fabric series where available (Tomber and Dore 1998) or the national Roman pottery reference collection at **http://potsherd.net/atlas/potsherd**, while a list of medieval ceramic reference collections is available in the Medieval Pottery Research Group's (MPRG) standards document (MPRG 2001) and on their website (**http://www.medievalpottery.org.uk/refcoll.htm**) (see also the specialist groups listed in **section 4**).

Clay compositions relate to their parent geology and can be useful indicators of the origins of the clay, but the fabric as a whole also reflects the potters' choices in raw material selection, paste preparation, vessel forming and firing (Day *et al* 1999, 1028) (see **case study 3**). Technological traditions, such as the use of particular clay paste recipes, vessel construction methods or decorative techniques, may be site specific, lasting for decades, or regional, even cultural, and be current for centuries.

Case study 3: interpreting pottery production technologies from thin sections

Anglo-Saxon cremation urns from Cleatham and Elsham, North Lincolnshire, from Perry (2013)

Pottery production in the early Anglo-Saxon period was very small scale. Potters exploited locally available clays, vessels were generally coil-built and fired in bonfires and/or pits, and finished pots rarely travelled far from their point of production to their point of deposition. In this study, thin sections of cremation urns were compared with thin sections of pottery obtained from surrounding domestic sites. The aim was to establish the provenance of the urns, enabling 'ceramic hinterlands' to be drawn around each cemetery, which in turn revealed the limit of each cemetery's catchment area (Perry 2013). Thus in this study, thin-section analysis was not used to answer pottery-specific questions but as a means of illuminating burial practice. The samples shown here (Fig CS3: A–D) highlight different production practices, for example the addition of different temper types and the identification of forming methods.

Anglo-Scandinavian Torksey ware, Torksey, Lincolnshire, from Perry (in prep)

Torksey ware was produced from the late 9th to late 11th century AD. Research has largely focused on chronological developments in form and decoration, and on determining the provenance of Torksey ware found at domestic sites by comparisons with kiln waste. The technological choices made by Torksey's potters have received less attention and the conclusions have been contradictory. Dunning (1959), for instance, believed that Torksey ware was wheel-thrown, while Barley (1964; 1981) claimed that it was coiled and wheel-finished. Although it is generally assumed that sand was added as temper to the potting clay, the source of this clay was unresolved, with two separate geological formations posited as potential sources.

Using thin-section petrology and geological sampling, the current study fully characterised the Torksey ware production sequence (Fig CS3: E–H), demonstrating that the potting clay was obtained from a source about 1.5km outside the village and that no temper was added because the clay was naturally sandy. Different clay was used to build the kiln superstructure, which was obtained at the kiln site. Analysis also revealed that Torksey ware was fully wheel-thrown and that the potters followed two distinct firing regimes. In the earliest kiln, pottery was fired in a reducing atmosphere to temperatures in excess of c 800–850°C. In later kilns, however, the pottery was fired at lower temperatures (below c 800–850°C) and, significantly, in an oxidising atmosphere, with a reducing atmosphere only in the final stages of firing (Perry in prep). Torksey ware emerged at a time when there was a revolution in ceramic technology, with a large-scale shift from coil-built, bonfire-fired pottery, to wheel-thrown, kiln-fired pottery. An awareness of these nuances in production provides important insights into the spread and ultimate success of these new technologies.

Provenancing English post-Medieval Slipwares, from White (2012)

Trailed and combed slipwares were manufactured at numerous production centres across England in the mid-17th and 18th centuries, but they appear remarkably similar in terms of fabric and decoration, and specialists often have difficulty telling them apart. Sherds from production centres in Bristol, North Staffordshire and South Yorkshire were compared using chemical and thin section analysis, to determine whether differences could be identified. The results showed that, even though there were shared technological traits, such as the blending of two clays (Fig CS3: I), the products of each production centre had distinct chemistries and textural arrangements that reflected specific workshop practices. The results demonstrated that these analytical methods, if applied more widely, could be useful in discriminating between slipwares manufactured in different centres.

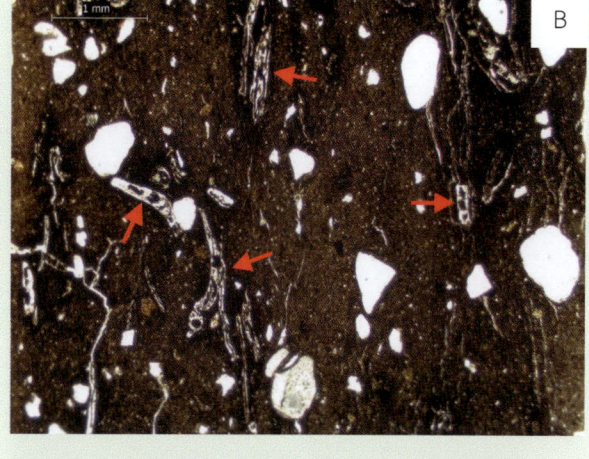
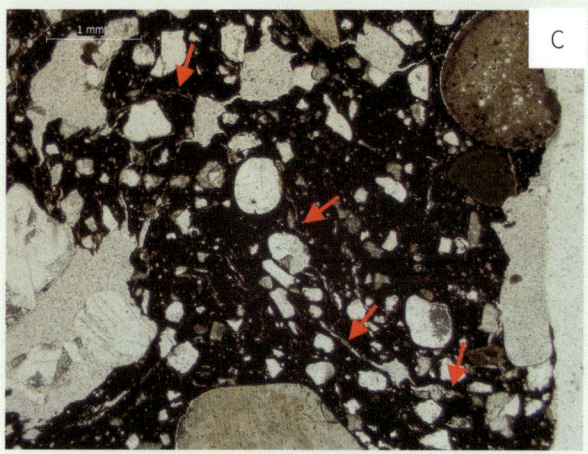
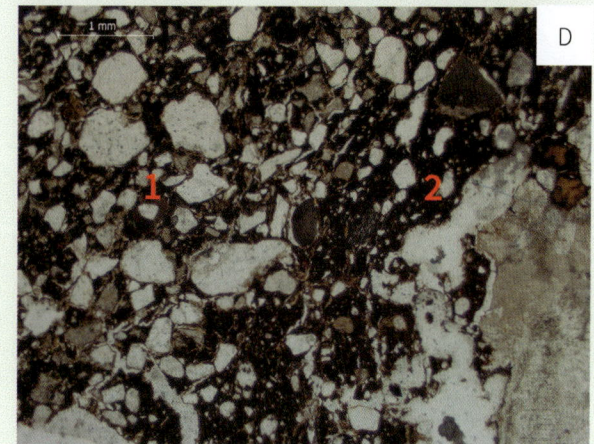
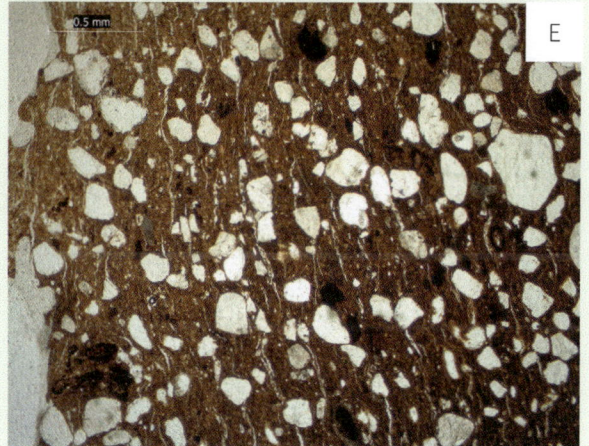

Figure CS3: A–E: All images XP = crossed polars. PPL = plane polarised light

A. The bimodal grain-size distribution (where both coarse and fine grains are present in equal frequency) shows that very coarse sand was used to temper the clay (Anglo-Saxon cremation urn, Elsham, North Lincolnshire) (width of image 6mm, XP).

B. The features highlighted by arrows are carbonised grass, showing this pottery was tempered with organic material, most likely dung (Anglo-Saxon cremation urn, Cleatham, North Lincolnshire) (width of image 6mm, PPL).

C. Coil joins may appear in thin section as an S-shaped void running from inner to outer surface, as picked out here (Anglo-Saxon cremation urn, Elsham, North Lincolnshire) (width of image 6mm, PPL).

D. Coils may also be detected by differences in texture if the clay is poorly mixed. The coil on the top left of this image (1) has more temper than the coil on the right (2) (Anglo-Saxon cremation urn, Cleatham, North Lincolnshire) (width of image 6mm, PPL).

E. Wheel-throwing is demonstrated by a preferred orientation of voids and inclusions in thin section. The voids here are linear and run parallel to the vessel walls (Anglo-Scandinavian Torksey ware, Torksey, Lincolnshire) (width of image 6mm, PPL).

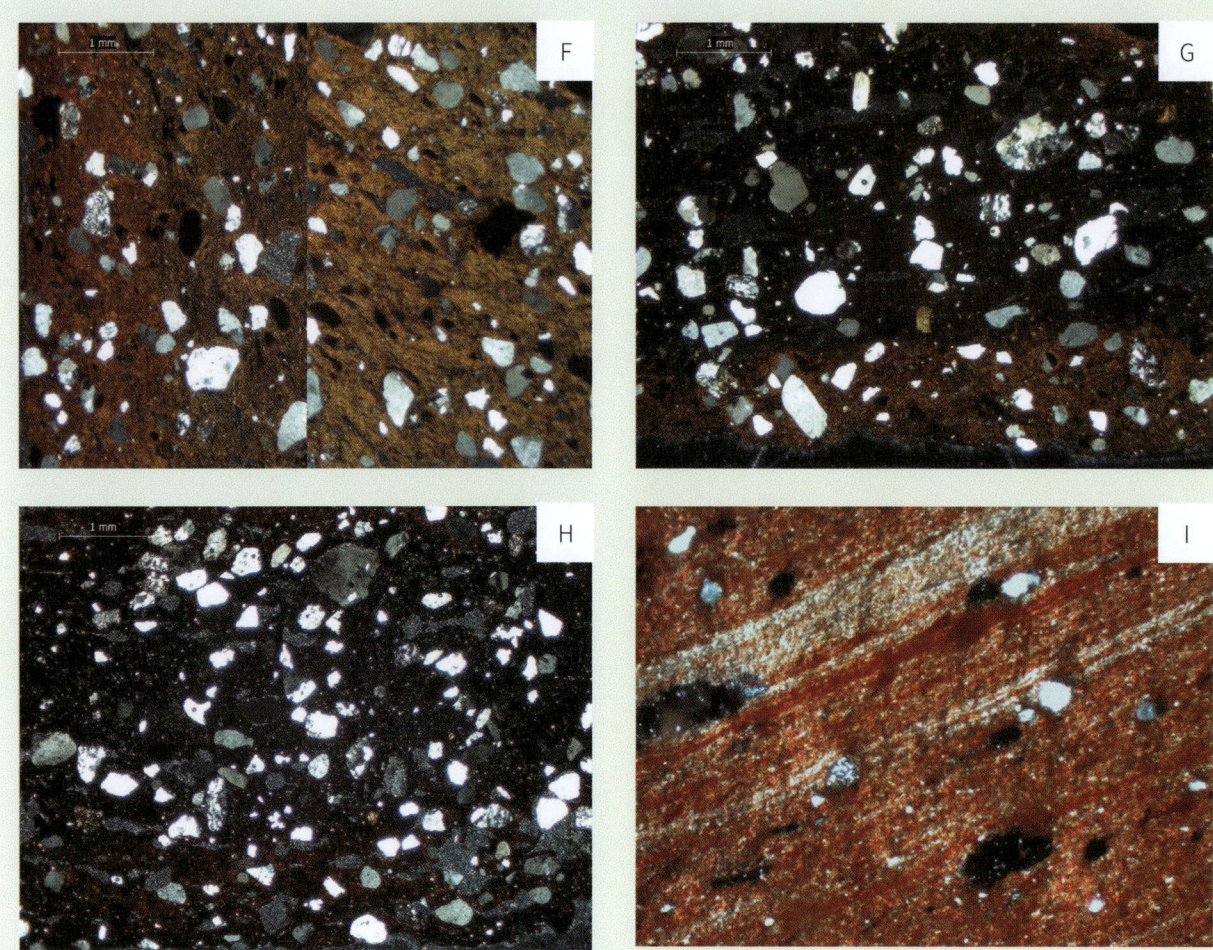

Figure CS3: F–I

F. Relative firing temperature can be determined by extent of optical activity. This Anglo-Scandinavian Torksey ware sample (Torksey, Lincolnshire) has a high optical activity; the clay domains change colour when the sample is rotated (compare the left and right sides of the image). The vessel was fired at <800–850°C, (width of image 6mm, XP).

G. This is a medium-fired version (fired at c 800–850°C) of the Anglo-Scandinavian Torksey ware fabric (Torksey, Lincolnshire) shown in Fig CS3: F. Like the low-fired example it has oxidised margins (brown) and reduced core (brown-black) but there is a significant difference in colour (width of image 6mm, XP).

H. This example of the Anglo-Scandinavian Torksey ware fabric (Torksey, Lincolnshire) was fired at a temperature >800–850°C. The clay domains are vitrified at this temperature, changing the appearance of the fabric matrix, and there is no optical activity on rotation of the sample (width of image 6mm, XP).

I. The lack of inclusions and presence of striations show the mixing of well-levigated pale and red clays (post-medieval slipware, Silkstone, South Yorkshire) (width of image 1.2mm, XP).

All figures in CS3 (except CS3: I): © Gareth Perry, Department of Archaeology, University of Sheffield, with permission from North Lincoln Museum, Scunthorpe and The Collection, Lincoln, The Viking Torksey Project. Figure CS3: I: © Harriet White

At production sites examples of the same fabric, especially in waster form, can appear superficially dissimilar, with different colours or levels of hardness even on the same pot; this is often the result of underfiring or overfiring, which makes wasters appear radically different in hand specimen, and so it is advisable that analysis is undertaken by an experienced ceramicist. Based upon the outcome of the initial assessment a subset of material should be selected for scientific analyses; chemical analysis or petrography can be used to confirm the validity of preliminary fabric groupings and these methods are given in **section 1.3.3**. There may also be large quantities of fragmented kiln structure and kiln furniture that will require sorting, recording and specialist study (Gregory 2004). In many cases the fabrics of kiln furniture and fragments of kiln superstructure are also described for comparison with the pottery itself.

Pottery assemblages from production sites may contain some pottery vessels that were used at the site by the potters but were actually made elsewhere. These wares will be less abundant and should have a different fabric to the pots made at the site.

1.3.1.2 Vessel form

Vessel form is established by studying the overall shape of a pot or by characterising its component parts. This subject is covered well elsewhere (MPRG 2001; Orton and Hughes 2013) but the method is especially important at production sites, where the range of fabrics is often very limited. Form analysis will characterise the products and provide comparative data for those working on consumption sites.

Pottery of the same fabric from a particular context is sorted according to vessel form, types of component parts, decoration and surface treatment, and quantified separately. If the assemblage has to be subject to selection, it is essential that multiple sherds exemplifying each different type of vessel, vessel component, decoration and surface treatment are retained in the archive (see sections 1.2.2.2 and 1.4).

- Vessel type: open or closed, the broad form category (eg jugs, jars, bowls) and overall shape (eg pear-shaped, hemispherical, straight-sided)

- Component parts: rims, spouts, handles, feet and body and base sherds, and how these are formed and attached

- Decoration: the technique used (eg applied, incised, stamped), the motif created and where on a pot it occurs

- Surface treatment: technique, placement, extent over a pot and sometimes colour

- Other marks, such as incised makers' symbols, pencil marks or other signifiers of lots or kiln loads

- Vessel size: production sites often produce complete profiles of pots, but rim or base diameter can also be used

1.3.2 Estimating the scale and organisation of production

Quantification follows the sorting of the pottery assemblage and should lead to an understanding of the output of the production site. The various quantification methods, including sherd count, sherd mass, estimated vessel equivalents (EVE) and number of vessels represented (eg minimum or maximum number of vessels) are described in detail elsewhere (Orton and Hughes 2013).

At pottery production sites the sherd count and mass are routinely recorded, together with either EVEs, or the absolute, minimum or maximum number of vessels. The EVE is a tool that provides an indication (rather than absolute measure) of how much of each pot is present in an assemblage, and can be particularly useful at a production site, where the range of fabric types is usually limited (see case study 2). Quantification can provide information on the relative breakage rates of different types of pottery, or different parts of a particular type of pot. Looking for adjoining sherds can also reveal more information about how the assemblage was deposited, as there may be cross-context joins. EVEs and the estimated number of vessels (ENVs) are more time consuming to produce, so different strategies may be adopted to deal with large assemblages with many thousands of fragments. At the Roman site of Newland Hopfields, Worcestershire, EVEs were only calculated for a proportion of the assemblage (see case study 2) (Evans et al 2000), and for the 11th-century Simpson's Malt site, Pontefract, West Yorkshire, additional resources were sought to assist with aspects of the process (see case study 1) (Cumberpatch et al 2013).

1.3.3 Further characterisation of the pottery

1.3.3.1 Technology

The technology of pottery making can be revealed by the study of associated objects, such as potting tools, turntables or wheels, raw materials, such as glazes, and also the pottery itself (Courty and Roux 1995). Analysis of the pottery should establish how it was made, for example hand-built, wheel-thrown, moulded or a combination of techniques. Characteristics such as colour, hardness and the types of firing failure (eg blistering, melting or bloating) will also indicate how well controlled the firing was, how the furnace atmosphere varied between oxidising or reducing and what sort of temperatures were attained (see case study 2). This is often easier to establish at a kiln site, where there will be partially finished pots, than with an assemblage from a consumption site. Sometimes it is possible to identify a type of pottery at a kiln site that is otherwise quite rare in the archaeological record, for example the wheel-stamped products of the 11th-century Simpson's Malt kiln, Pontefract, West Yorkshire (see case study 1) (Cumberpatch *et al* 2013).

Figure 7
Cross-hatching where a handle was attached to the side of a Romano-British vessel from Walbrook Valley, London, but the join failed during firing (Seeley and Drummond-Murray 2005).
© Museum of London Archaeology

Potentially distinctive technological traits might be useful in differentiating between potters or communities of potters. Pearce's (1984) study of handles on late 12th- to late 14th-century jugs found in London considered different handle shapes, how they were made and how they were attached to the jug (Fig 7).

1.3.3.2 Ceramic petrography

A number of samples from each fabric type identified in hand specimen should be analysed petrographically in order to understand fully the variability in clay paste recipes that may exist at a given site, as well as providing a more thorough description of the fabrics for comparative purposes. A slice from the pottery sherd is polished down to 30μm in thickness; thin section slides are typically 26mm × 46mm, which dictates the dimensions of the sample. The slide is examined using a transmitted-light microscope up to magnifications of ×400. The microscope is fitted with polarising filters; the sample can be viewed with one filter in place, known as plane polarised light (PPL), or using both filters, known as crossed polars (XP) (see case study 3). The technique is used to characterise the geological and technological attributes of a fabric. Subsequent reports or publications should include coloured photomicrographs of examples of typical fabric types that characterise products from a manufacturing site (see case study 3). This contributes substantially to the ease of comparison with similar wares recovered from consumer sites.

Mineral inclusions within the clay can be identified and related to the underlying geology of the area of origin. Clay preparation processes may be revealed in thin section by fabric textures and the grain size frequency distributions of the non-plastic components For example, clay refining methods, such as levigation, can be inferred from a truncation in coarse grain sizes or by a high proportion of fine-grained components. Additions of non-plastic temper can be reflected by a distinct bimodal grain size frequency distribution or by a high proportion of a coarse-grained component (see Figs CS3: A and CS3: B). Clay mixing can be detected by textural concentration features, such as clayey striations, or by clay pellets that appear to have been plastic during vessel fabrication (Quinn

2013, 151–71; Whitbread 1995, 392–3), while the addition of organic temper, such as chaff or grass, is indicated by characteristic voids left where plant material has burnt out during firing. Vessel-forming techniques, for example coiling or wheel-throwing, can be inferred from the orientation of voids and inclusions (Courty and Roux 1995; Rye 1981) (see **Figs CS3: C–E**), and relative firing temperatures can be determined by assessing the optical properties of the micromass (that is the fired clay matrix and fine silt component) (see **Figs CS3: F–H**).

Given the range of information that can be obtained from the study of ceramic fabrics, standardised methods for describing fabric thin sections are useful; for example, Whitbread (1995) specifies details of paste preparation, forming technique and firing regimes. Descriptions should include:

1. mineral and rock types comprising the non-plastic inclusions

2. the quantity, shape, size and grain size distribution of non-plastic inclusions

3. void type and orientation

4. textural concentration features such as striations or clay pellets

5. colour and optical activity of the micromass

1.3.3.3 Chemical analysis

Raw materials derived from different geological settings also have different overall chemical compositions, which can be determined using techniques such as inductively coupled plasma-atomic emission or mass spectrometry (ICP-AES/MS) (see **case study 4**). A small sample (c 0.2g) is obtained from each pot using a drill.

Case study 4: chemical analysis of pottery

From Paynter *et al* (2009)
Scientific techniques for investigating pottery include ceramic petrography (see **case study 3**) and chemical analyses [eg inductively coupled plasma (ICP) analysis and energy dispersive spectrometry (EDS)]. This case study focuses on the use of chemical analyses to determine where a particular fabric was made. Petrography is often used for this purpose with coarsewares because the large mineral inclusions identified in thin section are sometimes distinctive enough to indicate the probable origins of the fabric, eg Peacock's 1968 study of prehistoric pottery. Conversely chemical analysis tends to be more useful for finewares or fabrics with a fine matrix and an undistinctive, uniform temper.

Wasters from production sites are often used as controls for provenance studies (instead of, or in addition to, clay samples) because they provide a realistic indication of the composition and mineralogical make-up of the products made in a certain area at a particular point in time (see **section 1.3.3.3**). Chemical analysis can generate a large amount of data and statistical procedures are often used to investigate groupings more rapidly, for example using principal component analysis (PCA) (Haggarty *et al* 2011).

In this example, ICP analysis was used to investigate the production and distribution of Roman mortaria, later expanded to include other fabrics. The mortaria typically had a fine clay matrix and a quartz temper. The study focused on the Nene Valley, Cambridgeshire (Fig CS4: A), where there is evidence that mortaria were made in both the Upper and Lower regions of the valley, although the products themselves are difficult to tell apart. The mortaria from Mancetter–Hartshill, Warwickshire, are superficially similar so were analysed as well.

First, control groups were established made up of mortaria known to have been made in each of the areas. These sherds were from museum archives and were either wasters from kiln sites

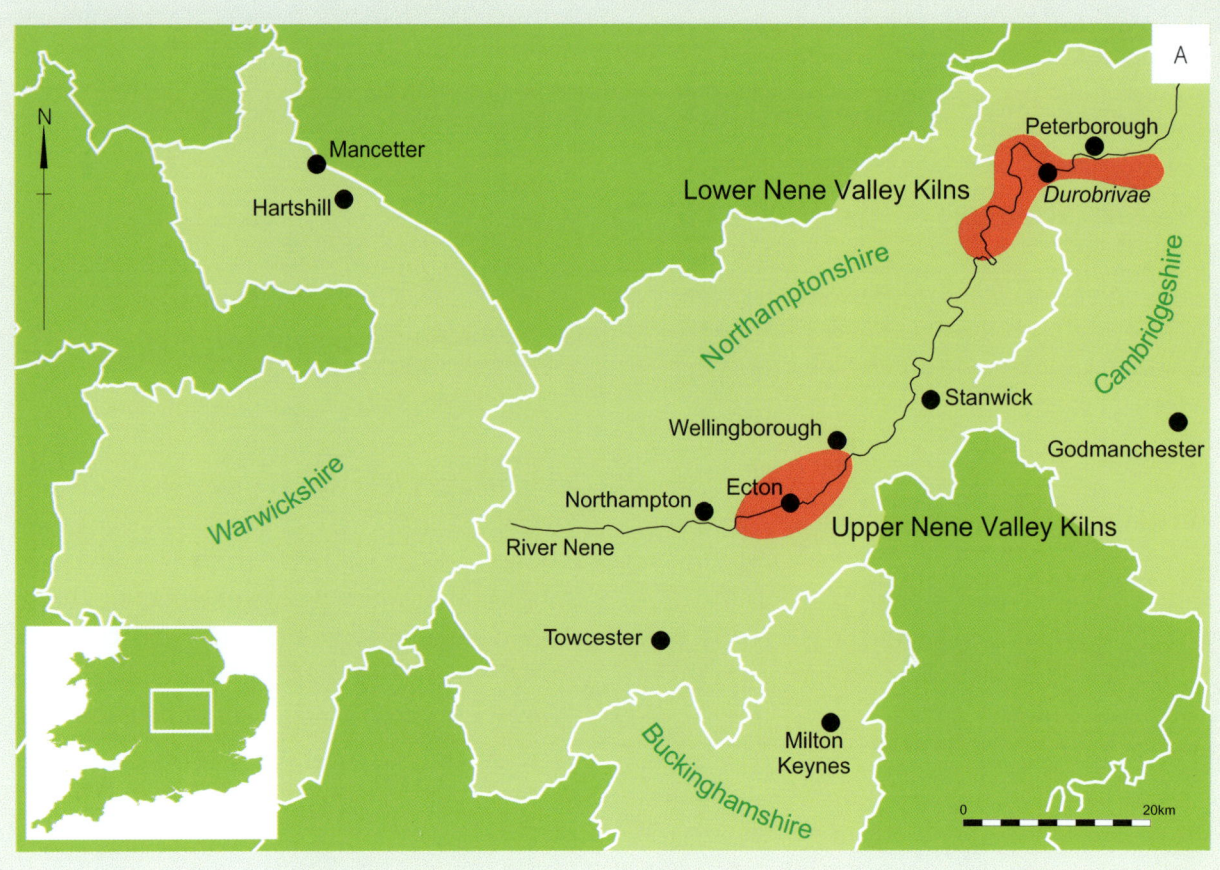

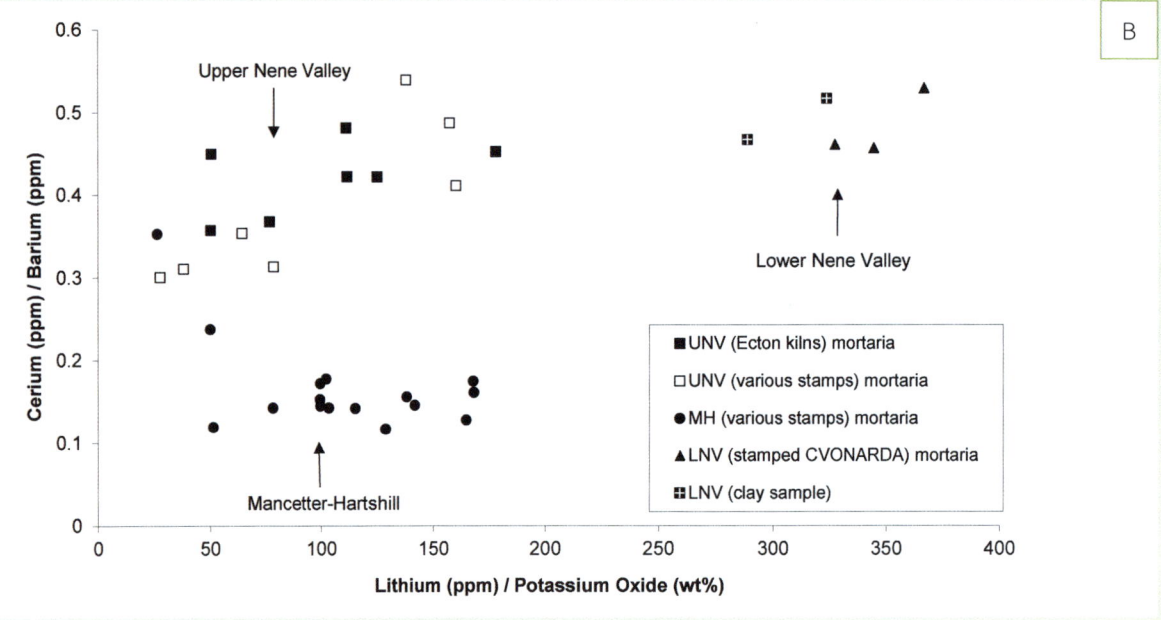

Figures CS4: A and B

A. Map of the production areas for the analysed mortaria, showing the Upper and Lower Nene Valley regions, Cambridgeshire, and Mancetter-Hartshill, Warwickshire.

B. Plot of element ratios comparing the control group mortaria (stamped or from kiln sites) from the three production areas: Upper Nene Valley (UNV), Lower Nene Valley (LNV), Cambridgeshire, and Mancetter–Hartshill (MH), Warwickshire (ppm = parts per million, wt% = percentage by weight)

or had a potter's stamp that indicated the place of manufacture. A minimum of 10 sherds was sampled for each control group, and the results compared to determine whether scientific analysis could differentiate the mortaria from the three production areas. Second, a proportion of the hundreds of mortaria excavated at the Romano-British settlement at Stanwick, Northamptonshire, was analysed in order to determine where they were made and so understand the patterns of supply to Stanwick from the mid-2nd to the mid-3rd centuries AD.

The results for the control groups showed that the mortaria from each area could be identified. The mica-rich fabric of the Mancetter–Hartshill mortaria was easily differentiated from the Nene Valley products, by ICP and also by thin-section analysis. ICP analysis was able to differentiate between mortaria produced in the Upper and Lower Nene Valley, even though they were indistinguishable in thin section (Paynter et al 2009 (Fig CS4: B)). A comparison with published analyses of different clay sources near the kiln sites established that the Nene Valley mortaria, and some other Nene Valley coarsewares, were made using local Upper Estuarine Series clay. The composition of this clay changes very little throughout the Nene Valley, with the exception of a few diagnostic elements, but all of the Stanwick coarseware fabrics made from this clay could be assigned to a place of origin based on the concentrations of these elements in the pottery. Mortaria from the Upper and Lower Nene Valley, plus Mancetter–Hartshill, were all found to be well-represented at Stanwick.

Scientific analysis can be used to identify and describe pottery fabrics from any period, site or region; however, the archaeological interpretation of these groups, such as determining where fabrics were made and their chronological sequence, is largely dependent on the retention of adequate archives from pottery-production sites.

Chemical analysis can be particularly useful for characterising finewares where petrography is less useful because the inclusions are too small to identify. It is also helpful in areas where there are multiple kiln sites, exploiting deposits that are too similar to be distinguished petrographically but where there may still be subtle chemical differences. Standards of known composition should be analysed with the pottery, to ensure the quality of the results.

It can be useful to sample and analyse clay from potential geological sources and storage pits at a pottery production site for comparison; however, even if these were used in production, they may not closely match the composition of the ceramics because of the techniques used by the potters that alter the composition, such as levigation, the addition of temper and clay mixing. Instead it may be more straightforward to find a match for a particular fabric (from a consumption site) by comparing it with products from contemporary kiln sites making the same type of ware.

A number of different fabric types might be produced at one kiln site, either simultaneously or over a period of time, and so the output of a single production site may be represented by more than one chemically distinct group. Conversely, similar types of ware may be produced by contemporary kilns in different areas, which can be distinguished using chemical analysis (see case studies 1 and 4). At least ten samples from each fabric group identified in hand specimen need to be analysed to produce statistically significant compositional groupings. Technological attributes identified in thin section may help explain any variability encountered, for example quartz-tempered samples will be more silica-rich, with diluted concentrations of everything else.

The results can be explored using multivariate statistical techniques, most commonly agglomerative hierarchical clustering and principal component analysis (PCA). These methods sort, group and describe sets of material according to their chemical similarities. It is essential that reports contain all of the compositional data collected for the pottery, and also the standards analysed at the same time, rather than just charts, averages or summaries, so that other researchers can compare results in full.

1.3.3.4 Scanning electron microscopy

Scanning electron microscopy (SEM) can be used to examine samples at very high magnification. An SEM normally has an attached analytical facility, such as an energy dispersive spectrometer (EDS), allowing small features to be analysed at the same time, although this is not as sensitive as the other analytical methods already described.

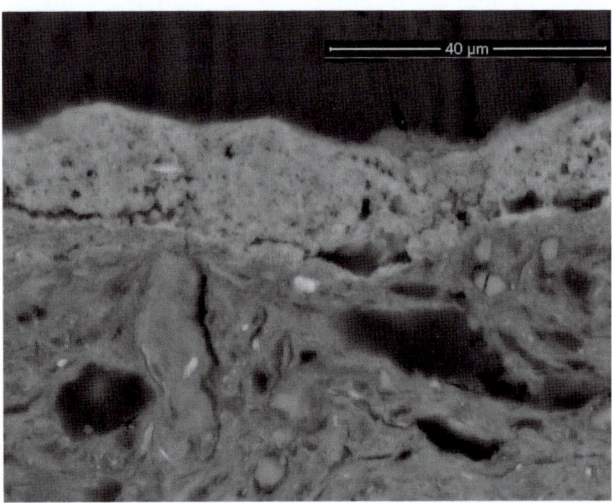

Figure 8
Scanning electron microscope image of a Neolithic pottery sherd from Marden, Wiltshire, showing a very thin (around 10 microns) coating on the surface of the vessel (the light grey layer at the top of the image).

Electron microscopes are most useful for examining microstructures and compositions of surface coatings such as glazes, slips and pigments (Fig 8), in addition to identifying silt-sized mineral inclusions within ceramic bodies that are too small to be examined with transmitted light microscopy alone. Automated EDS can be used to map the mineralogy of a sherd and distinguish between the composition of the matrix and the inclusions using specialist software packages. An SEM can also be used to estimate firing temperatures, where the microstructure of a sherd is compared with subsamples of the same sherd refired at different temperatures.

1.3.4 Documentary, ethnographic and experimental resources

There are many aspects of pottery production in the past that are difficult to investigate from the archaeological record alone, for example how the labour was divided, the status of the potters in their community and the rituals that were associated with pottery production.

Documentary sources can provide some of this information, especially for later periods (see **section 1.1.2.2**). Ethnographic studies of potters working with a wide variety of methods in different parts of the world also offer fresh insight into all aspects of potters' practices and can aid the interpretation of archaeological evidence (Fig 9) (Peacock 1982). In addition to published studies (Gosselain 1999; Sillar 2000), photographs and films of potters at work can now be found online. Experimental work can establish the practicality of a proposed kiln reconstruction, the types of evidence left by particular practices and how glaze recipes behave (Fig 10) (Dawson and Kent 1999).

1.4 Archive

Beyond current national and international standards for creating and compiling archives from any archaeological project (eg Brown 2011; Perrin *et al* 2014), repositories of archaeological material, principally museums, will have their own requirements for the creation, selection, packing, ordering and transfer of archive material. The appropriate repository for the project archive should be identified in the project planning and their requirements understood from the outset.

Pottery production sites often present a challenge for repositories because the quantities of finds can be very large, so curators should be consulted when the selection strategy is being developed and when any variation to that, or any other procedures, is discussed. They should also be included in discussions of how to destroy or discard material that is not to be retained within the project archive. It is not recommended that decisions on retention are made solely because of the size of the finds assemblage or the space

Figures 9 and 10
09. Charamoray, Peru: a potter grinding talc to be used as a temper (Sillar 2000, 55).
© Bill Sillar
10. A reconstruction at Bickley of the early 17th-century kiln 2 from site 13 of the Donyatt potteries, Somerset.
© David Dawson, Oliver Kent and the Bickley Ceramics Project

available within a store; selection must be guided by the potential of the archive to inform future research and support community projects.

Samples of new or unrepresented types should be offered to local, regional and national ceramic type series and reference collections (MPRG 2001) (see section 4).

Material selected for archive must include the full range of material recovered, including pottery, kiln furniture, kiln structure and raw materials. Classes of material must be considered on a case-by-case basis rather than selecting material according to arbitrary percentages. The material retained will act as a type series of illustrative examples, but must also include a statistically representative sample of the site assemblage overall, which can be used for future analysis or study. Unusual or rare objects, such as tools or equipment used in manufacturing, should all be kept, as should complete objects, including pots.

Particular consideration should be given to the curation of digital material, including data gathered from scientific analysis. Many museums or similar repositories are not equipped to curate digital files, and national and international standards stipulate the use of a trusted digital repository. The Archaeology Data Service (ADS) is currently the only such repository in the UK that curates archaeological data and has developed online guidelines for digital archive compilation and transfer (http://archaeologydataservice.ac.uk).

1.5 Preservation of pottery production sites

The case for preserving remains at ceramic production sites is dependent on factors such as the degree of preservation and the significance relative to other contemporary examples, regionally and nationally. The appointed specialist should be consulted for more detailed advice on a case-specific basis with reference to regional frameworks (see section 4). Surviving production sites, kilns and their associated buildings are rare, however, and as such are important industrial heritage assets (Pearson 2011). There are a small number of extant examples in England, generally 18th century or later in date; the regional studies by Baker (1991) and Dawson and Kent (2012) provide some examples from the West Midlands and the south-west, respectively.

Case study 5: Middleport Pottery

From The Prince's Regeneration Trust (2012)

Bottle kilns are distinctive structures that reflect the industrial heritage of an area. They were developed in the early to mid-18th century, and were initially relatively small, for example as at Dunster, Somerset (see Fig 11), but became progressively larger, until they were producing pottery on a massive scale; the internal oven could hold thousands of pieces of pottery at any one time stacked in saggars (English Heritage 2006b, 8) (see Fig 20). The Clean Air Acts of the 1950s and the introduction of continuous-firing gas and electric kilns meant that by the 1970s bottle kilns were obsolete, resulting in the loss of hundreds across the country. Intact bottle kilns are now rare, particularly those in their original location with associated buildings. Surviving kilns may still be at risk; the recent English Heritage Industrial Heritage at Risk project showed that listed industrial buildings are more at risk than any other kind, and the collapse of the hovel over the surviving bottle kiln (Grade II listed) at the Falcon Works, Hanley, Staffordshire, in early 2012 reinforces this point.

The Middleport Pottery Regeneration Project demonstrates how the preservation of standing industrial remains can be integral to the regeneration of an area and, as at the Gladstone Museum, Longton, Staffordshire, become a focal point for industrial heritage education. Middleport Pottery, Port Street, Burslem, Stoke-on-Trent, Staffordshire, was purpose-built as a 'model pottery' in 1888–1889 for Burgess and Leigh, where all production processes could be housed on one plot. The works consisted of a slip house, potters' workshops, printers' and decorators' workshops, three bottle kilns for biscuit firing and a further four for glost firing, glost warehouses and a packing house. It was sited adjacent to the Trent and Mersey Canal for ease of receiving raw materials and exporting

Figure CS5: A
Profile tools at Middleport Pottery, Stoke-on-Trent, Staffordshire.

© The Prince's Regeneration Trust

finished wares. Burleigh ware, the blue and white transfer-printed ware for which it is famous, was produced at the works from 1903.

Middleport Pottery changed hands and was developed over the next century, one of the most significant changes being the introduction of gas-fired tunnel kilns in 1949 and 1951. Following the Clean Air Act of 1956, six of the seven bottle kilns were decommissioned and demolished. Crucially, the seventh bottle kiln survived because it was structurally integral to its adjacent building. Middleport Pottery continued to produce Burleigh ware using traditional methods throughout the 20th century. In 2009 the Middleport Pottery was faced with the risk of closure. At this time the site comprised numerous significant buildings and a substantial archive of equipment and machinery associated with the traditional production methods of blue and white transfer-printed ware, such as a steam engine, moulds, bowl-making equipment and a copper plate printing press.

The Prince's Regeneration Trust bought the Grade II* listed site in 2011 and, with financial support from English Heritage, the Regional Growth Fund, European Regional Development Fund and the Heritage Lottery Fund amongst others, has started a programme of renovation and regeneration at the site. The project aims to restore the Grade II* listed buildings, preserve the bottle kiln, drying tower, steam engine and machinery collection, and catalogue the extensive mould collection and production process archive (Figs CS5: A and CS5: B). Following the restoration works, the site will be used for businesses, crafts and heritage education. The public will be able to go inside the bottle kiln, which will be bought to life with an audio-visual interpretation. Pottery production continues at the site, preserving Middleport's unique status as the last Victorian pottery using traditional methods in the UK.

Figure CS5: B
The former mould store at Middleport Pottery, Stoke-on-Trent, Staffordshire.

© The Prince's Regeneration Trust

For upstanding kiln remains, recording will help to inform future management, development or designation decisions, to document the remains in case of loss or damage, and to promote understanding. The level of recording will vary in accordance with the project aims and necessity, but will generally include descriptions of building typology and condition, associated machinery and fixtures, and factors influencing the significance of the site, all of which may draw on documentary, photographic and other sources as necessary (English Heritage 2006d; 2011b; The Prince's Regeneration Trust 2012). Some features maybe suitable for photogrammetric recording, and three-dimensional (3D) images of kilns have been created successfully.

Sites can be safeguarded in many ways, such as positive management, policy and designation, and a variety of approaches have been taken towards kiln sites depending on the circumstances. Preservation *in situ* may be the most appropriate course of action, in accordance with national planning policy (NPPF 2012). Significant kiln sites have been preserved in their original locations and many of these are scheduled, such as the Romano-British examples at Sloden Inclosure, New Forest, Hampshire (Swan 1984), and the 18th-century Dunster kiln, Somerset (Dawson and Kent 2012) (Fig 11).

Many later kilns, and their associated buildings, have been adapted to other uses, commonly as craft centres and heritage museums, for example 19th-century Middleport, Staffordshire (see **case study 5**), 19th-century Swadlincote, Derbyshire, and 19th-century Bridgwater, Somerset. In some cases the development proposal has been adapted to safeguard archaeological evidence of pottery production, as at the 19th-century Grimshaw pottery site, Lancashire (Oxford Archaeology North 2012) and at Southwark Cathedral, London, where the remains of a 17th-century tin-glazed kiln are on permanent display (Divers and Jarrett 2008). On occasion kilns have been dismantled and re-erected, as with the 18th-century Bovey Tracey salt-glazing kiln, Devon, and the mid-17th-century kiln remains at Barnstaple, North Devon, which were excavated

Figure 11
The 18th-century kiln at Dunster, Somerset.
© David Dawson

and relocated to the Museum of Barnstaple and North Devon (Dawson and Kent 1999).

Guidance on conservation planning and recording is provided by Gould (2008). Advice on conservation and management options for industrial remains can be found on the Historic England website (**https://www.HistoricEngland.org.uk/advice/heritage-at-risk/industrial-heritage**).

2 Evidence of Pottery Production

This section describes in more detail the types of evidence that might be found at a pottery production site, including firing areas, kilns, kiln furniture, pottery wasters, workshop structures (such as settling tanks), pottery-making equipment and tools, and dumps or spreads of raw material and fuel for firing.

2.1 Pottery kilns

2.1.1 Open firings, clamp firing and pit firing

The simplest pottery firing technology was open firing (also called bonfire firing). In open firings, pottery was stacked on a bed of fuel on the ground, with more fuel placed amongst, around and over the pottery (Fig 12). Variations included covering the fuel/pottery mound with an insulating material such as turf or broken pottery (clamp kilns or clamp firing) or stacking the pottery within a low-walled structure (Best *et al* 2013; Orton and Hughes 2013).

In Britain, open or clamp firing was the main firing method used from the Neolithic through to the Late Iron Age and during the Anglo-Saxon period until around the 9th century AD. Even when updraught kilns otherwise dominated, clamp kilns continued to be used occasionally, particularly for specific ceramic industries such as brick or tile manufacture (Drury 1981).

Archaeological evidence for open firing is notoriously limited because no superstructure is required, firing durations are short and the temperatures reached are relatively low. Thus open firing remains are difficult to distinguish

Figure 12
Totorani, Bolivia: open firing with stacked pottery covered in llama dung and dried grass. Broken cooking pots form a windbreak around the edge of the firing (Sillar 2000, 64).
© Bill Sillar

from other hearth remains (Fig 13), and the low-fired, coarse nature of much prehistoric pottery in Britain does not produce easily identifiable wasters. There may be a high proportion of burnt sherds, however, and potentially types of firing furniture, as at Late Bronze Age Tinney's Lane, Sherborne, Dorset (Best *et al* 2013). The use of open firings during this period is

Figure 13
Raqchi, Peru: a patio floor after dismantling an open firing with dung fuel, showing oxidation in the centre of the clay-rich surface, surrounded by carbon deposition and reduction where a wall of loose stones contained the firing area (Sillar 2000, 65).
© Bill Sillar

primarily interpreted through the appearance and characteristics of the pottery itself (Varndell and Freestone 1997). Similarly, surface kilns, constructed and operated with portable kiln furniture, are likely to be difficult to recognise.

Possible Neolithic clamp kilns have been identified at Allt Chrisal, Barra, Outer Hebrides, in an area characterised by a number of hearths of different designs. The first hearth consisted of burnt soil, ash, charcoal dust, pottery sherds and blocks of baked turves, structured in a way that suggested the disturbed covering of a clamp kiln. The second was demarcated by an area of small stones and comprised structured deposits of orange/red burnt soil containing charcoal flecks, with lines of burning, again indicating the remnants of turf blocks (Branigan and Foster 1995, 85–8). The remains of probable Late Bronze Age bonfire firings were also identified at Tinney's Lane, Sherborne, Dorset, where burnt stone features were found with concentrations of broken or burnt pottery nearby, and also unusual perforated clay objects that are potentially a type of kiln furniture (Best *et al* 2013).

2.1.2 Updraught kilns

The Late Iron Age/early Romano-British period saw the introduction of updraught kilns in Britain; with updraught kilns, the hot gases from the burning fuel are drawn up through the chamber containing the pottery. Updraught kilns continued to be developed throughout the Romano-British period. Subsequently there was a reversion to open or clamp firings, before updraught kilns were reintroduced in the middle Anglo-Saxon period; by the late Anglo-Saxon period updraught kilns were again widespread.

Most updraught kilns were circular or oval in plan, although some large rectangular or square variants were also used, such as the Romano-British examples recorded at Colchester, Essex, and Brampton, Norfolk, or the 17th-century tin-glaze industry at Montague Close, Southwark, London (Dawson 1971; Seeley and Drummond-Murray 2005; Swan 1984).

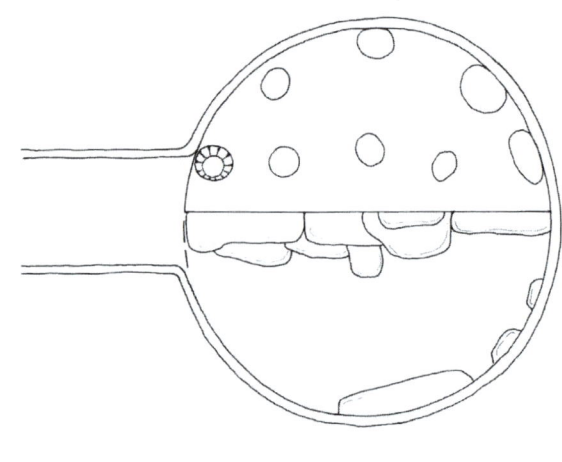

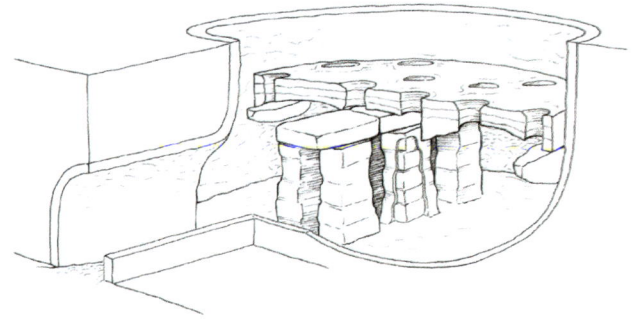

Figure 14
Reconstruction of a Romano-British updraught kiln from Walbrook Valley, London; sectional plan (above) and sectional reconstruction (below) (Seeley and Drummond-Murray 2005).
© Museum of London Archaeology

The simplest kilns had one or more stoke pits where fuel was fed into flues or fireboxes; the hot gases from the burning fuel rose through the ware chamber, where the pots were stacked, escaping through the top of the kiln. Often there is evidence of a means of raising the wares up from the floor, for example by making a platform from arranged kiln bars, or by constructing a raised perforated floor, effectively creating a combustion chamber beneath and a ware chamber above (Fig 14). Evidence for raised supported floors may be difficult to discern, however, and mistakenly removed.

The methods and materials used to construct updraught kilns were variable, and not all types would leave substantial or easily recognisable archaeological remains. As updraught kiln technology developed in Britain, kiln structures became more significant, with walls and internal features such as chamber floors and floor supports constructed out of more durable materials, including stone, fired clay, bricks, tiles and pottery wasters (Fig 15).

It is not always easy to recognise and interpret the structural elements of archaeological kiln remains; inferring kiln type can be difficult if truncation is severe. A more detailed guide to identifying the different elements of a kiln is given in sections 2.1.2.1–6.

2.1.2.1 Stoke pits and ash pits

The stoke pit is where fuel was fed into the kiln and excess ash and charcoal raked out. It may appear as a depression dug into the ground at the entrance to a firing chamber. Stoke pits may be oval or circular in shape and variously have steep sides, sloping sides or can be stepped. With coal-fired kilns there is generally a grate, where the coal was burnt, with an ash pit beneath. Deposits within the stoke pit or ash pit may contain fuel residues (eg charcoal, ash or clinker), as well as material cleared from other areas of the site after the kiln ceased to be used.

2.1.2.2 Flues or fire boxes

Simple updraught kilns may have tunnels dug into the subsoil, lined with clay, stone, tile or brick,

Figure 15
A well-preserved 14th-century updraught kiln at the Teardrop site, Woolwich, London, where London-type ware was produced, featuring a central pedestal that would have supported a raised ware chamber floor, and two flues/fireboxes.
© John Cotter and Oxford Archaeology

leading from the stoke pit into the combustion chamber. These are often referred to as flues, and sometimes as fireboxes, in order to differentiate them from the flue systems in more complex kilns of the post-medieval period and later, which were brick-built passages used to channel hot gases into, and sometimes through, the kiln (see also section 2.1.2.6).

The dimensions of flues and fireboxes can vary and are not dependent on kiln type. An example is Romano-British kiln 918 at Heath Farm, Postwick, Norfolk, where there was simply a fired clay arch approximately 0.12m in length attached to the combustion chamber. At the same site, however, a second kiln had a much longer, 0.9m, clay-lined flue or firebox connected to the combustion chamber (Bates 2003a).

Deposits within flues or fireboxes may contain fuel residues and provide evidence of kiln reuse. Swan (1984, 128) highlighted the case of a Romano-British kiln excavated at Sloden Inclosure, New Forest, Hampshire, that contained several layers of ash within the flue or firebox separated by layers of silt representing periods of successive firing and disuse; there was also evidence the walls had been relined. Post-medieval and later kilns, such as bottle kilns, are large structures; their substantial foundations and any underground portion of the flue system often survive (see sections 2.1.2.6 and 2.1.3).

2.1.2.3 Ware and combustion chambers

It can be difficult to determine whether remains are the base of a combustion chamber, where truncation has occurred below the floor level of the ware chamber, or the base of the ware chamber, where fuel combustion occurred in an adjoining flue or firebox. There are a number of possible features that may help to establish which is the case: for example, if there was a raised ware chamber, there should be evidence for some sort of floor support in the form of impressions or features on the chamber base that may indicate the position of a pedestal, tongue support or similar structure. It is important to be aware that if the remains of pottery vessels, sometimes clay encrusted, survive in the base they may be the floor support for a raised ware chamber, rather than representing the *in situ* remains of the final load.

Examination of kiln waste dumped in other areas of a site may also provide an indication of kiln type. For example, the presence of fire bars or fragments of characteristic perforated fired clay would indicate that a kiln in the vicinity had a raised floor.

If the floors or walls of the kiln chamber were clay, the internal surfaces will have been highly fired and so are more likely to survive, whereas the extremities will have been exposed to less heat and so are less likely to survive; this means it can be difficult to discern the true thickness of clay structural features. Careful consideration should be given as to whether clay was used in conjunction with other materials, such as turves, soil or wasters.

2.1.2.4 Superstructure

Kiln superstructures rarely survive archaeologically. Although parts of the collapsed or demolished superstructure are sometimes recovered from inside kilns during excavation, it is extremely difficult to reconstruct their form because of the fragmentary nature of the remains.

Many possible arrangements for kiln superstructures have been considered, including permanent free standing domes, temporary domes, permanent open-topped kilns with near vertical walls and a temporary capping, and open-topped kilns (Dawson and Kent 1999, 2008; Musty 1974; Swan 1984).

It may be possible to determine whether the kiln walls were constructed out of materials such as brick, stone or tile, and there may be wattle impressions from a supporting frame. Surviving inner walls should be examined (eg by a fired clay specialist) for evidence of repair, such as relining or clay patching, which would indicate the kiln had been used more than once. An *in situ* collapsed kiln superstructure can be compared with suspected fragments from other contexts, to help establish the source of dumped waste.

2.1.2.5 Kiln shelters

There may be evidence of shelters, windbreaks or protective buildings for the kiln, although surviving evidence of this is rare before the post-medieval period (Fig 16); examples include the postholes surrounding a number of medieval kilns at Harefield Lane, Nuneaton, Warwickshire (Mayes and Scott 1984, 37), the series of stakeholes around the sides and upper edges of the stoke pit of one of the Romano-British kilns at Heath Farm, Postwick, Norfolk (Bates 2003a), and the circular structure built around the early 16th-century opposing flue/firebox kiln at Donyatt, Somerset (McCarthy and Brooks 1988).

In later periods some industrial kilns were covered with a free-standing, bottle-shaped chimney called a hovel (see section 2.1.2.6 and case study 5) but many kilns were incorporated into conventional buildings, which served as

Figure 16
A reconstruction of the Romano-British kilns and workshop at Walbrook, London (Seeley and Drummond-Murray 2005).

© Museum of London Archaeology

cover for firing as well as providing space to dry wares (Dawson and Kent 2008).

2.1.2.6 Variants of updraught kiln

Swan (1984, 55) describes Late Iron Age examples of surface, or slightly sunken, updraught kilns, typically with circular or oval firing chambers and one, or rarely two, flues/fireboxes and stoke pits. Survival of this type of updraught kiln is generally poor so evidence found during excavation is often in the form of a 'dumb-bell'-shaped footprint of burning.

Into the Romano-British period, the majority of kilns had raised ware chamber floors supported by a variety of methods, including built-in tongue supports extending from one side, cross-walls or corbels, or portable pilasters, pedestals or up-turned pots; chamber floors were either continuous and perforated, or constructed out of bars that radiated from the central support to the edge (see **Figs 14** and **15**). A type of muffle kiln was used for some specialised wares, where the hot gases from the fuel were contained within flues as they were channelled through the ware chamber.

A variety of medieval kiln variants have been identified (Musty 1974), with different numbers and arrangements of stokeholes and fireboxes/flues and with or without raised floors (Fig 17). In the post-medieval and later periods there were a number of developments of the updraught kiln (classified by Dawson and Kent 2008) that enabled the introduction of coal as a fuel and ultimately led to the bottle kiln (see **Figs 11** and **18**).

Figure 17
The 17th-century kiln 3 at Potters Lane, Barnstaple, North Devon, under excavation.

© David Dawson

The bottle kiln is a development of the updraught kiln, introduced in the 18th century and continuing in use until the mid-20th century in Britain. One variant had a distinctive bottle-shaped cover building, known as a hovel, that protected the domed kiln enclosed within and acted as a chimney, helping to control the draught (Barker and Goodwin 2006, 8; Dawson and Kent 2008). There was also a system of flues directing hot gases. The muffle kiln was a further specialised variant for glost (glaze) firings or firing whitewares. In muffle kilns the wares were separated entirely from the damaging effects of flames and combustion materials, which were drawn up through the kiln in a system of sealed flues. In the commonest type of bottle kiln, the chimney is raised on top of the ware chamber (see Fig 18).

2.1.3 Downdraught kilns

Downdraught kilns were developed in the 19th century. In these the hot gases from the fireboxes were directed towards the top of the kiln and deflected down through the chamber before being vented through low-level flues to a chimney (see Fig 18). Although these kilns can appear superficially similar to contemporary updraught kilns, they can be distinguished by the arrangement of fireboxes and flues. In downdraught bottle kilns the portion of the flues under the chamber floor radiates out between the fireboxes, rather than connecting with them, and so the fireboxes do not need to be constructed at a level below the chamber floor (Dawson and Kent 2008, 204–5).

2.2 Kiln furniture

The term 'kiln furniture' describes portable firing aids used to help stack, separate and protect the pots in the kiln during firing; 'setters', 'separators' or 'stackers' were used to separate vessels horizontally or vertically within the loaded kiln. Many different forms of setters have been identified and include rings, short cylinders, clay wedges, rolls of clay, and flat, roughly circular plates with central perforations (Swan 1984, 38–40). Waster sherds, slate and tiles were also used.

Setters were particularly important for firing glazed wares, because glazes become molten at high temperatures and easily fuse with adjacent vessels. From the medieval period onwards tripod stilts with fine pointed feet were used to separate glazed plates or dishes (Gregory 2004) (Fig 19).

Figure 19
Some of the kiln furniture from the early 19th-century Cambrian Pottery, Swansea, including pipeclay trivets, ring-shaped spacers and setters, small cockspur trivets and some moulded clay lumps and saggar fragments.
© John Cotter

Glazed wares sometimes have impressions from stilts left on their inner surfaces, rims or bases, which indicate how the vessels were stacked in the kiln. From the 18th century many specialised types of setter were developed.

Smaller vessels could be loaded into larger ones for ease of stacking; special ceramic containers called saggars later served the same purpose (Fig 20). There are different variants: the tin-glazed industry used round saggars with vertical rows of triangular peg holes, with pegs, in which to stack plates for glazing, some saggars were completely sealed to protect the vessels inside and to control the localised atmosphere, whereas those for glazing stoneware had large openings cut out of the side to ensure the circulation of salt vapour (Divers and Jarrett 2008; Tyler *et al* 2008).

2.3 Pottery wasters

Pottery wasters are vessels that were misfired or damaged during firing and are one of the primary signifiers of a pottery production site. If overheated, the vessels could become bloated with surface bulges, or dunted, where they slumped and deformed. Occasionally, whole stacks of vessels have been found collapsed and

Figure 18
An updraught kiln converted to downdraught at East Quay, Bridgwater, Somerset, with characteristic bottle-shaped chimney and added square chimney. The kiln produced ornamental bricks and tiles in the 19th century.
© David Dawson

fused together [see case study 2 and Fig CS2: A]. Prehistoric pottery wasters are harder to identify although they may be burnt on the outside or show evidence of spalling (Best *et al* 2013); alternatively they may be underfired. Pottery wasters are an important category of artefact at pottery production sites because they provide direct information on production processes. They also help fix pottery types to a production centre, which is a crucial initial step in pottery provenance studies.

Other causes of firing failure that would lead potters to reject wares include underfiring, especially in the case of glazed wares, where glazes have not reached a sufficiently high temperature to form properly, as found at medieval Hanley Swan, Worcestershire (Hurst 1994, 121), or cracking and shattering as a result of too rapid changes in temperature, particularly if the vessels have not been dried thoroughly before firing.

In other high-temperature industries, such as glass and metalworking, failed products were recycled back into the melt. Although pottery wasters could be incorporated into kiln structures as building material, or ground up and added to clay as grog temper, most were generally discarded and, depending on the duration and scale of production, could accumulate in significant quantities.

Wasters are often found in dumps or spreads near kilns, or filling ditches and pits nearby. Large amounts were often backfilled into kilns after they went out of use. Wasters were also sometimes used in the construction or loading of the kilns. Therefore the wasters found inside a kiln were not necessarily made in that particular kiln, and may not be contemporary with the kiln or each other (Divers and Jarrett 2008). Occasionally waster dumps have been found without any trace of a kiln, either because it does not survive or it is outside the excavation area, but examination of the wasters and kiln furniture can still provide valuable information.

2.4 Fuel waste

The types of fuel used to fire pottery kilns varied according to what was available. Wood was commonly used, so ash- and charcoal-rich residues are often encountered at production sites. Analyses of charcoal waste from in, and around, kiln structures have shown that potters used mixtures of different woods and plant materials depending on what was found nearby.

The Romano-British kilns at Two Mile Bottom, Norfolk, for example, were situated adjacent to heathland and were fired primarily using heather with smaller quantities of oak, hazel and rowan/hawthorn and cereal waste, while the Romano-British kiln at Elingham, Norfolk, approximately 55km to the east, was fired using oak, alder and cereal waste (Bates 2003b). Peat was also used as fuel for pottery kilns; it produces a much smaller flame than wood and so would have required a greater number of fireboxes to maintain heat in the kiln. It is thought that the medieval kilns with multiple fireboxes (or flues) of Toynton All Saints, Lincolnshire, were fired using peat dug from nearby fenlands (McCarthy and Brooks 1988; Stocker 2006). In areas such as Yorkshire and the Midlands, coal became the main fuel type used; coal produces a characteristic vitrified ash called clinker, which is dark in colour, porous and lightweight.

2.5 Buildings and related features

Various different structures or features can indicate a pottery production site, including workshops, storage for raw materials and fuel, and sheds or other areas for drying unfired vessels and storing finished products. The excavation and identification of these features can reveal much about the workshop organisation and working practices of past potters (see Figs 1 and 16). Workshops would probably have been constructed according to local contemporary building traditions (eg stone, cob, wattle and daub).

Some ethnographic studies have suggested that a drying time of days or weeks would have been necessary between forming and firing pots

Figure 20
The kiln setting, with saggars and typical stoneware products in the foreground, at Price, Powell and Co., Thomas Street, Bristol, c 1940.

© Bristol Museums, Galleries and Archives

Figures 21
A Romano-British clay settling pit at Plumley Wood Quarry, Hampshire.

© Thames Valley Archaeological Services

(McCarthy and Brooks 1988, 40). Pots could be dried more rapidly near a fire or in a chamber adjoining a kiln, although drying must often be carefully controlled. Structures may have been constructed to protect drying vessels from the weather, and pots could have been arranged on planks or racks to improve circulation of the surrounding air. In many societies pottery-making activities, such as the digging of clay, drying of pots and burning of fuel, are seasonal, and confined to drier and warmer periods (McCarthy and Brooks 1988), although Gibson and Woods (1997, 44) point out that pottery production is still feasible in winter.

Structures used for drying and protecting pottery need not have been substantial and may have had multiple uses, so archaeological remains can be ephemeral and difficult to identify. Drying sheds may contain evidence of a source of heat, such as hearths. T-shaped dryers are known (Moorhouse 1981, 104) and also more complex systems such as the Romano-British hypocaust at Holt, North Wales (Swan 1984, 47–8). Medieval posthole structures at Limpsfield, Surrey, have been interpreted as possible examples of drying chambers, making use of the heat from adjacent kilns (Moorhouse 1981); however, evidence for how pots were dried can sometimes be found on the vessels themselves (Seeley and Drummond-Murray 2005).

2.6 Raw material extraction, storage and processing

Cobbled or packed-clay working floors, where clay was mixed, often by treading, have been found. Constructed floors may have had different purposes, for example cobbled platforms excavated on either side of a kiln at medieval Olney Hyde, Buckinghamshire, are thought to have been fuel stands for wood used during firing (Moorhouse 1981, 104).

Clay and other raw materials, such as sand for temper, were prepared and stored at pottery production sites. Tips of clay, sand and shell were uncovered at the production site at late Anglo-Saxon Silverstreet, Lincoln, Lincolnshire, which produced mainly shell-tempered jars or cooking pots (Miles *et al* 1989). Deposits of clay and burnt flint for temper were also found amongst Bronze Age production waste at Bestwall, Wareham, Dorset (Ladle and Woodward 2009).

Pits are a common feature on production sites and could have served a variety of purposes, including the extraction of raw materials, puddling clay and storage (Fig 21). Stone-lined pits used for clay preparation have been found at several pottery production sites, for example at Romano-British Stibbington, Cambridgeshire (Wild 1973), medieval Lyveden, Northamptonshire (Moorhouse 1981), and post-medieval Wrenthorpe, Warwickshire (Moorhouse and Roberts 1992). At Stibbington, one of the pits was filled with clay mixed with a temper of ground-up freshwater mussel shell. Levigation systems for clay refining have also been identified, for example the arrangement of interconnected pits joined to a water channel excavated at Romano-British Trent Vale, Staffordshire (Mountford *et al* 1968).

At post-medieval and later sites, equipment powered by water, then steam, was used for stirring and grinding raw materials (Fig 22). While this equipment rarely remains, the footings for the machinery may survive (Fig 23) (Palmer *et al* 2012).

2.7 Equipment and tools

A wide variety of equipment and tools used for preparing raw materials, and forming, finishing and decorating vessels, are known from archaeological sites, although they are infrequent finds. Many of them were made of perishable materials and most were portable and thus not necessarily discarded when production sites were abandoned (Hamilton 2002).

- Querns were used to crush or powder raw materials such as temper, or ingredients for glazes

- Socketed stones have been recovered from several Romano-British production sites and are interpreted as pivot stones for potters' wheels (eg Bates and Lyons 2003, 90; Swan 1984, 50–1)

- Vessel moulds, or more probably mould fragments, may also occur. Romano-British examples are known from the Samian factory at Colchester, Essex (Hull 1963), at York, North Yorkshire, and at Littlemore, Oxfordshire (Young 1971). Moulds were also used in the production of post-medieval and later pottery (Dawson 1997)

Figure 22
20th-century blunger at Burgess and Leigh, Middleport Pottery, Burslem, Stoke-on-Trent, Staffordshire.
© Historic England Archive

Figures 23
The blunger room at the site of the 19th-century Barton Hill Pottery, Bristol, looking west.

© Bristol and Region Archaeology Services and David Dawson

Smaller hand tools used for finishing and decorating vessel surfaces have also been found (Fig 24), including the following.

- Knives and sheep bones (leg and foot) found at medieval Lyveden, Northamptonshire (Moorhouse 1981), were probably used for trimming vessels and forming rims

- Rounded pebbles may have been used for burnishing vessel surfaces, and a possible example of a burnishing stone was identified at Romano-British Meole Brace, Pulley, Shropshire (Evans et al 1999)

- Combs and scribes used for incising the surface of leather-hard vessels may occur in a variety of materials. One example is a sharpened antler point from Romano-British Two Mile Bottom, Norfolk (Bates and Lyons 2003, 90)

- Shaped and worn pottery sherds may have functioned as potters' ribs (eg late Anglo-Saxon Lincoln, Lincolnshire; Miles et al 1989)

- Dies or stamps, used to impress complex decorative motifs, including rosettes and faces, have been found at a number of medieval sites. There are carved antler points from mid-Anglo-Saxon Hamwic, Southampton, Hampshire (Timby 1988) (Fig 24)

Figure 24
An Anglo-Saxon antler pot stamp excavated from the Six Dials site in Hamwic, Hampshire.

© Southampton City Council Arts and Heritage

3 Background Information on Pottery Production in England

3.1 Raw materials

There are many suitable clay deposits available in Britain (Simco 1998; 2000). Different factors influence a potter's choice of clay, such as the clay's properties, the location of the deposit and the ease of transporting it. In later periods, improvements in transport meant that clays with particular properties could be brought from far afield; in the 18th century, china clay from Cornwall and plastic clays from Devon and Dorset were utilised nationally by the wider ceramic industry (Dawson 1997, 200–5).

A potter is unlikely to use the clay as dug; it will first be prepared by weathering, kneading, trampling, levigation or sieving, and then may be mixed with another type of clay, or temper, for example crushed or burnt rock, gravel, sand, shell, plant material, dung and grog (crushed pottery) (McCarthy and Brooks 1988). The addition of temper changes the properties of the clay during working or use. In very broad terms, earlier Neolithic pottery was often tempered with flint or stone, whereas grog was more common in the later Neolithic and earlier Bronze Age (Woodward 2002). Later Bronze Age and Iron Age pottery was more diverse, with a clearer distinction between coarseware and fineware. Grog tempering was also used in the Roman period, for example it was widespread throughout Hampshire, Sussex and Kent. In the Anglo-Saxon period a range of tempers were used, such as organic material, sand, gravel and rock, with variation both chronologically and regionally (Gibson and Woods 1997). Some clay already contains material that can act as a temper, such as fossil shell, so it can be difficult to distinguish between intentionally added temper and inclusions that have occurred naturally in the clay deposit.

3.2 Manufacture

3.2.1 Hand-building

Pottery is hand-built in many different ways, for example by coiling rolls of clay on top of each other (coil building), or by joining slabs (slab building), strips or rings of clay, then scraping or pressing the joins together (Gibson and Woods 1997; McCarthy and Brooks 1988; Varndell and Freestone 1997, 32–7). Evidence of the type of construction is occasionally seen in sherds, from fracture patterns or where joins have not been completely obscured, and is often easier to detect in wasters from production sites. It may also be noted in thin section by linear voids running diagonally between the inner and outer surfaces of a sherd, or by textural differences between the coils (see case study 3) (McCarthy and Brooks 1988, 22). Pots can also be made by pinching, pulling or pushing the clay, either by hand or using the paddle and anvil technique (McCarthy and Brooks 1988, 11).

Before the 1st century BC, virtually all pottery produced in Britain was hand-built. All early Anglo-Saxon pots were also hand-built, either by coiling and drawing or by pinching or slab building. Specialist ceramic objects are often hand-built, regardless of the period. Some hand-built pots were finished on a turntable, adding a rim or decoration. Evenly finished rims, often with a clearly visible join to the body of the pot and well-executed decoration, are indicators of the use of a turntable. Evidence of construction techniques is often more obvious in wasters from kiln sites, for example the examination of medieval material from excavations at Lyveden, Northamptonshire, led to the realisation that the pottery was coil-built (Moorhouse 1981).

3.2.2 Wheel-throwing

A wheel made it easier, and potentially quicker, to form symmetrical pots with thin walls and smooth surfaces. Potters' wheels are likely to have varied by period, region and purpose, such as turntables, wheels that were set rotating by hand, foot or stick, manually powered wheels or mechanised belt-driven wheels. A combination of hand-building and throwing, or use of a turntable, was used to shape some pottery; pots were also often made as composites, adding hand-formed feet, handles or decoration to wheel-thrown vessels.

Imported wheel-thrown continental pottery is known from some 2nd-century BC sites in England but local production of wheel-thrown pottery is not seen on any scale until the 1st century BC in south-eastern Britain (Hamilton 2002; Hill 2002). In the Romano-British period some pottery was produced by wheel and other types by hand. Stone objects that may have acted as flywheels or kickwheels have been found at Romano-British pottery production sites; the one shown in Figure 25 has lead-filled holes on one side to balance it and wear patterns on the other side (Swan 1984).

Figure 25
A Romano-British potters' kickwheel from a well at Stibbington School, Huntingdonshire.
© Historic England Archive

A number of wheel-thrown industries appear in the 9th century AD (Vince 1993) although, in parts of Anglo-Saxon England, hand-building remained the favoured method until well after the Norman Conquest. By the middle of the 13th century, the wheel had been widely adopted, especially among industries producing on a larger scale (McCarthy and Brooks 1988).

Indications that a vessel was thrown include a characteristic spiral ribbing on the vessel surface, especially on the inside, the regular alignment of voids and inclusions, cutting-off marks on a flat base and sometimes horizontal decoration added as the wheel rotated (McCarthy and Brooks 1988, 21). Archaeological or historical evidence for potters' wheels is rare, although there is a probable pivot-and-kick wheel from Stibbington School, Huntingdonshire, of Roman date (Fig 25) (Swan 1984, 50–1), and a few depictions of potters using wheels appear in medieval manuscripts.

3.2.3 Moulding

Moulding is a quick and secure method for the repeated reproduction of identical forms, and suits pottery manufacture on a large scale. Simple forms, like bowls, could be made in a one-piece mould, but complex forms required more pieces. Thin sheets of clay could be pressed into, or slumped over, a mould, a pot could be thrown within a mould or an object could be cast in a mould by pouring in a clay slip. Moulds were used to form pots in the Roman period, most notably at the Samian factories in Gaul, and for lamps and finewares with relief decoration. Lightly fired earthenware moulds have been found at Roman sites producing Samian-type wares, such as Colchester, Essex, and also for moulding face-masks on jugs (Swan 1984, 52). Moulded vessels are occasionally found in atypical fabrics, from as yet unidentified production centres (Bulmer 1980). Roman and medieval tiles and bricks are thought to have been made with wooden moulds containing sand as a release agent to prevent the clay from sticking to the mould (Middleton 1997, 158–63; Pearson 2011). Moulds were also used in post-medieval and later industry; from the 17th century, hump moulds were widely used for flatware production and from the 19th century both the hollow and hump moulding processes were mechanised using jigger and jolley machines. Slip casting was used in later periods (see case study 5 and Fig CS5: B).

3.3 Decoration

Leather-hard clay is well-suited to decoration using burnishing, rustication, fettling, incising or impressing, using fingers or other materials such as cord, nuts, textile and unmodified bone, to form patterns or shapes (see Fig 24); for example, a cattle toe bone was used to make an impressed motif at 15th/16th-century Hanley Swan, Worcestershire (Hurst 1994). Purpose-made dies, stamps or roulettes (roller stamps), made from antler, bone, stone, wood, fired clay or metal, were used for more complex motifs (Fig 26). Shaped pieces of clay could also be added, from simple pads to complex anthropomorphic or zoomorphic forms, for example the knight jugs made in Yorkshire in the 13th century, where models of free-standing knights on horseback were fixed around the body.

Figure 26
A Bronze Age beaker from Oxfordshire, with incised and impressed decoration.
© The Trustees of the British Museum

Figure 27
A fragment of 18th century pottery, about 30mm long, from the production site at Temple Back, Bristol, with a feathered, trailed slip decoration covered in a lead glaze.
© Harriet White

Slips could be applied when the clay was leather-hard, by hand-smearing, brush, trailing and dipping, to give a coloured, sometimes glossy, surface finish after firing (McCarthy and Brooks 1988). The first slips appear in the Late Bronze Age. Many Roman finewares were coated in an iron-rich slip, applied by dipping, which gave a red colour when oxidised-fired, or became black when reduction-fired (Roberts 1997, 188–93); subsequently the practice of dipping pots in slips may not have been common until the 16th century (McCarthy and Brooks 1988, 35). Highly decorated forms of pottery were developed during the late 12th and early 13th centuries, and some 13th- and early 14th-century vessels were very elaborate, with slips in complex painted motifs, incised decoration and lead glazes. Tools were developed for applying slip more precisely, such as cow horns or small pots fitted with a quill or reed (Gaimster 1997a). Complex designs were created using the *sgraffito* technique (see **Fig 5**) or by combing trailed colours to produce a feathered pattern (Fig 27).

Pigments were also used for decorative effect; some of the earliest examples are the white calcium carbonate infill in the decoration of pre-Iron Age beakers, and the haematite (iron oxide) rubbed into the surface of Early Iron Age pots to produce a glossy red finish on firing. Pigments were sometimes used to colour clay or slips, for example cobalt oxide was added to the clay body of Wedgwood's famous blue Jasper ware.

3.3.1 Glazes

The lead-glazed pottery of the Roman period, coloured in shades of green to amber, is the earliest made in Britain (although these colours appear in later periods as well). Lead glazes reappear in a few places in the late Anglo-Saxon period and probably became commonplace by the end of the 11th century (see **case study 1**). Good extensive glazing on the interior of pots does not become widespread until the post-medieval period, although glazes are found on the internal bases of earlier, mainly open, forms. The glazed products of the 10th century AD, notably Stamford- and Winchester-type wares, exhibit yellow or pale sage-green lead glazes, perhaps brushed, smeared or dipped using a suspension in water (McCarthy and Brooks 1988) (Fig 28). Glazes typical of the 12th and 13th centuries often appear pitted and were probably produced by applying a lead flux to the clay before firing (Newell 1995). From the 13th century, it was more common for glazes to be applied as a

Figure 28
Huayculi, Bolivia: pouring a lead-glaze suspension over a pot with incised decoration, with glazed but unfired pots in the foreground and fired-glazed pots to the left (Sillar 2000, 66).
© Bill Sillar

liquid suspension, sometimes by dipping the pot. Deposits of sand and lead carbonate were found at the 15th-century kiln site of Chilvers Coton, Nuneaton, Warwickshire (McCarthy and Brooks 1988), whereas at the 15th- or 16th-century Hanley Swan kiln site, Worcestershire, lead oxide or lead carbonate was applied directly to the clay and fired to form a glaze (Hurst and Freestone 1996).

Salt glaze was created by shovelling raw salt into a high temperature kiln and was therefore common on stoneware, which was not made in England until the late 17th century, although many stoneware vessels were imported before then (Gaimster 1997b, 176). Stoneware could be decorated before firing by painting pigments onto the pottery surface, often blue (cobalt) but also purple (manganese) and brown (iron) (Gaimster 1997b, 122–7). Archaeological evidence for the 17th-century production of stoneware has been found at Woolwich and Fulham, London. At the latter, the remains of multiple kilns plus a settling tank for clay and a sand pit were discovered (Green 1999).

Tin-glazes are white and opaque, perfect for painted decoration using coloured pigments or metallic lustre. Tin-glazed wares were not made in England until 1568 in Norwich and London, but imports from Europe are found prior to this (Fig 29). Archaeological evidence has been found for the production of tin-glazed earthenware in the 17th century, for example in Southwark, London, near the site of the Pickleherring pottery kiln (Tyler *et al* 2008). Large assemblages of kiln waste include broken vessels with a friable white coating of unfired glaze (Paynter 2000).

3.4 Firing

The ideal firing temperature for a particular clay depends on the make-up of the clay, which also influences the colour of the fired pot, depending on how the atmosphere in the kiln varies during firing. Dawson and Kent (1999, 164–7) describe the typical variation in atmosphere during a firing cycle in a simple updraught kiln, from oxidation to reduction to reoxidation, and the various ways this cycle can be controlled to determine the colour of the ware and its decoration. A possible archaeological example of controlling the kiln atmosphere was recorded at Romano-British Stibbington in the Nene Valley, Cambridgeshire (Wild 1973), where one of a pair of 4th-century AD kilns had been used for producing greywares. The flue/firebox of the former kiln was intentionally obstructed and sealed with debris to maintain a reducing atmosphere while the wares cooled.

Plant matter in clay can affect the colour of the fired pottery (Haith 1997, 151). Fine particles of carbon can also deposit on the surface of pottery during firing if the atmosphere surrounding the pot is very smoky or if the pot is in contact with charring fuel in a bonfire firing.

Figure 29
18th-century, tin-glazed wasters from Wincanton, Somerset.
© David Dawson

4 Where to Get Advice

4.1 Further reading

Study groups for pottery from different periods have produced frameworks for research (Irving 2011; Perrin 2011) as well as comprehensive guidance for processing, recording, analysing, publishing and archiving pottery (Darling 1994; MPRG 2001; PCRG 2011). A list of ceramic reference collections is available in MPRG's standards document (MPRG 2001) and on their website (http://www.medievalpottery.org.uk/refcoll.htm).

Orton and Hughes (2013) provide a full overview of pottery studies, while Gibson and Woods (1997) and McCarthy and Brooks (1988) provide more detailed introductions to prehistoric and medieval pottery, respectively.

Swan (1984) and Musty (1974) describe kiln types of the Roman and medieval periods, respectively. Dawson and Kent (2008) focus on the bottle kilns of the post-medieval and later periods, and Baker (1991) on the bottle kilns of Staffordshire, while Palmer et al (2012) provide an overview encompassing the extractive industries as well.

Barclay (2001) and Quinn (2013) describe how scientific analysis can be applied to pottery.

4.2 Specialist advice

Historic England science advisors are based in local offices and are available to provide independent, non-commercial advice on all aspects of archaeological science. For contact details see http://www.HistoricEngland.org.uk/advice/technical-advice/archaeological-science/science-advice/ (section 4.6).

Currently there is no one source for finding active pottery specialists. However, contact details of consultants are available from the Chartered Institute for Archaeologists (CIfA) and the pottery research groups Medieval Pottery Research Group (MPRG), Study Group for Roman Pottery (SGRP) and Prehistoric Ceramics Research Group (PCRG) (see section 5.3). Most scientific analysis of pottery takes place within the archaeological science or archaeology departments of universities; again information is available via the science advisors, the pottery research groups and university websites.

4.3 Organisations

Association of Local Government Archaeological Officers (ALGAO)
http://www.algao.org.uk
This association provides a forum representing archaeologists working for local authorities and national parks throughout the UK.

Chartered Institute for Archaeologists (CIfA)
http://www.archaeologists.net/
This group provides general information, including standards, on the practice of archaeology and allied disciplines.

Institute of Conservation (ICON)
http://www.icon.org.uk/
This group represents those concerned with the conservation of cultural heritage in the UK. The site includes the Conservation Register of accredited conservators/restorers and a range of guidance material.

Medieval Pottery Research Group (MPRG)
http://www.medievalpottery.org.uk
A group with an interest in pottery vessels and ceramic building materials between the end of the Roman period and the 19th centuries, from both sides of the Atlantic and beyond.

Prehistoric Ceramics Research Group (PCRG)
http://www.pcrg.org.uk/
A group specialising in prehistoric pottery, covering ceramics from the Neolithic and earlier Bronze Age periods, and incorporating the previous Iron Age Pottery Research Group and the First Millennium BC Ceramic Research Group.

Study Group for Roman Pottery (SGRP)
http://www.romanpotterystudy.org
A group with the aim of furthering the study of pottery from the Roman period in Britain.

4.4 Datasets

Archive of Anglo-Saxon Pottery Stamps
http://www.aasps.org.uk/History.html
An archive of the known stamp impressions on hand-made pottery from Britain, between AD 400 and AD 700. The website includes a link to the Archive of Roman Pottery Stamps (ARPS), recording stamp impressions on wheel-turned pottery from the fourth century in Britain, plus stamps from Iron Age and earlier Roman pottery from Britain when found.

Gallo-Belgic pottery database
http://gallobelgic.thehumanjourney.net
A website devoted to Gallo-Belgic pottery (terra nigra and terra rubra) found in Britain, including a digital record of potter name stamps and marks.

South Yorkshire/North Derbyshire medieval ceramics reference collection
http://archaeologydataservice.ac.uk/archives/view/ceramics_eh_2003/
A resource containing descriptions, photographs, petrographic and chemical information on primarily medieval pottery from the county of South Yorkshire and the northern part of Derbyshire.

The pottery kilns of Roman Britain
http://mapdata.thehumanjourney.net/vgswandb_map.html
An online gazetteer of Roman pottery kilns, based on the work of Vivien Swan.

Worcestershire online ceramic resource
http://www.worcestershireceramics.org/
A comprehensive pottery fabric series for Worcestershire, with an incorporated form type series.

4.5 Museums, collections and resources

Middleport Pottery, Stoke-on-Trent
http://www.princes-regeneration.org/middleport-pottery/visit-us
A website that contains information about the traditional methods of pottery production still used at Middleport, and a summary of the history of the site, which includes a bottle kiln, Victorian offices and a large mould store.

Museum of London: the ceramics and glass collection
http://www.museumoflondon.org.uk/ceramics/pages/ceramics.asp
An online database including catalogue records of the ceramic items in the Museum of London collection, together with descriptions of the main ware types.

Potweb
http://potweb.ashmolean.org/
An online catalogue for the ceramic collection of the Ashmolean Museum of Art and Archaeology.

The Museum of Barnstaple and North Devon
http://www.devonmuseums.net/The-Museum-of-Barnstaple-and-North-Devon/Devon-Museums
The website for the museum, which houses the largest public collection of North Devon Art pottery and the remains of a 17th-century kiln.

The Potteries Museum
http://www.stokemuseums.org.uk/
A joint website for The Potteries Museum, the Etruria Industrial Museum and Gladstone Pottery Museum.

Wedgwood Museum
http://wedgwoodmuseum.org.uk/learning/virtual-etruria
A website with a virtual tour of the Wedgwood factory as it would have appeared around 1900, plus archive film of various pottery production processes.

4.6 Contact Historic England

East Midlands
2nd Floor, Windsor House
Cliftonville
Northampton NN1 5BE
Tel: 01604 735400
Email: eastmidlands@HistoricEngland.org.uk

East of England
Brooklands
24 Brooklands Avenue
Cambridge CB2 2BU
Tel: 01223 582700
Email: eastofengland@HistoricEngland.org.uk

Fort Cumberland
Fort Cumberland Road
Eastney
Portsmouth PO4 9LD
Tel: 023 9285 6704
Email: fort.cumberland@HistoricEngland.org.uk

London
1 Waterhouse Square
138-142 Holborn
London EC1N 2ST
Tel: 020 7973 3000
Email: london@HistoricEngland.org.uk

North East
Bessie Surtees House
41-44 Sandhill
Newcastle Upon Tyne
NE1 3JF
Tel: 0191 269 1200
Email: northeast@HistoricEngland.org.uk

North West
Suites 3.3 and 3.4
Canada House
3 Chepstow Street
Manchester M1 5FW
Tel: 0161 242 1400
Email: northwest@HistoricEngland.org.uk

South East
Eastgate Court
195-205 High Street
Guildford GU1 3EH
Tel: 01483 252000
Email: southeast@HistoricEngland.org.uk

South West
29 Queen Square
Bristol BS1 4ND
Tel: 0117 975 0700
Email: southwest@HistoricEngland.org.uk

Swindon
The Engine House
Fire Fly Avenue
Swindon SN2 2EH
Tel: 01793 414700
Email: swindon@HistoricEngland.org.uk

West Midlands
The Axis
10 Holliday Street
Birmingham B1 1TG
Tel: 0121 625 6820
Email: westmidlands@HistoricEngland.org.uk

Yorkshire
37 Tanner Row
York YO1 6WP
Tel: 01904 601901
Email: yorkshire@HistoricEngland.org.uk

5 Glossary

Biscuit (bisque) firing The first firing of pottery, before a glaze is added.

Bloating When clay is overfired to the extent that it melts, blisters and distorts.

Blunger A piece of equipment, consisting of a tank and mechanised stirrer, used for mixing clay and water.

Bottle kiln A kiln with a bottle-shaped chimney.

Burnishing Giving the clay a shiny surface by polishing it, commonly with a pebble, before it is completely dry.

China clay A pale-firing raw material, rich in the mineral kaolinite.

Clamp firing Firing pottery in a fire without a permanent superstructure, but covered with an insulating layer such as turves or wasters.

Coarseware Pottery containing large inclusions.

Coil building A method of hand-building pots, by shaping clay into rolls and winding them around on top of each other, before smoothing them together to form a continuous surface.

Downdraught kiln From the 20th century, a type of kiln where the hot gases rise up from the firebox, are deflected down from the roof, through the load, then out through flues and a chimney.

Earthenware Pottery fired within a lower temperature range, normally less than about 1100°C, which remains porous.

EDS Energy dispersive spectroscopy, used for chemical analysis.

ENV Estimated number of vessels, a method of quantifying pottery.

EVE Estimated vessel equivalent, a method of quantifying pottery.

Fabric The term given to the material from which a pot is made, commonly described in terms of the range of colours, composition and textures of the clay, and the type, size and frequency of inclusions, either naturally occurring or deliberately added as temper.

Fettling Finishing or smoothing the surface of a leather-hard clay object.

Fineware Pottery made using clay with a fine particle size and the large inclusions removed.

Firebox The component of the kiln where the fuel is burnt.

Firing The process of heating a clay object causing irreversible changes to the clay and driving out inherent moisture, making it hard and brittle.

Flue A tunnel or passage that hot gases travel through.

Flux A material that lowers the melting point of another substance, such as a lead-fluxed glaze.

Frit Made by partially firing, then crushing, the raw materials to be used for glazing, in a process known as fritting.

Glaze A thin glassy coating melted on to the surface of a clay object during firing.

Glost firing A firing for melting the glaze.

Grog Ground-up pottery used as a temper in new pots.

Hand specimen A sample of pottery, usually an unprepared fragment or sherd, chosen for examination by eye.

Hovel A cover building, often bottle-shaped, protecting a kiln or oven within, and helping to produce an even draught.

Hump mould A plaster mould used for forming tableware.

ICP Analytical techniques using inductively coupled plasma, which are capable of detecting very low concentrations of many elements.

Jigger/jolley Machines for making tableware, comprising a rotating plaster hump mould or hollow mould combined with a profile, which came into use during the 19th century.

Kaolin A type of white, stoneware clay, also known as china clay.

Kiln bars Bars made of fired clay that could be used to construct a raised firing chamber floor.

Kiln furniture Items used to help stack or protect wares in the kiln, including stackers, setters, trivets, saggars, props and spacers.

Lead glaze Glaze fluxed with lead oxide, which could be made using a variety of lead compounds, eg galena.

Leather-hard A partially dry vessel that is firm but not brittle.

Levigation Using water to separate the finer particles of clay from the coarser ones.

Lustre A metallic effect decoration, mainly on tin-glazed wares.

Muffle kiln A kiln used for some specialised wares, where the hot gases from the fuel were contained within sealed flues as they were channelled through the ware chamber.

Open firing Firing pottery in a bonfire, with no superstructure.

Oxidised firing Firing in an oxygen-rich atmosphere in the kiln, which causes reddish-orange colours to develop in iron-bearing slips or clay.

Paddle and anvil A method for hand-forming pots, using one implement to support the pot inside (the anvil) and the other (the paddle) to beat the outside of the pot.

Paste Plastic, prepared (levigated, mixed, tempered, etc) clay from which vessels are formed.

Petrography A scientific method for characterising pottery fabrics, using a light microscope and polarised light to identify the minerals present in a thin section of the pottery.

Plastic Describing the deformable properties of wet clay.

PPL Abbreviation for plane polarised light, when using one polarising filter during optical petrography.

Reduction firing Firing in a low-oxygen atmosphere, which causes iron-bearing clays and slips to develop a grey to black colour.

Roulette Roller stamps used to produce a repeating decorative pattern on the surface of pots.

Rustication Roughening the surface of a pot with random marks, often done using fingers.

Saggar A ceramic vessel or box used to protect pots (especially glazed ones) during firing and provide a means of packing the kiln; the pot is fired inside the saggar.

Salt-glazing A method of glazing stoneware by introducing salt into the kiln at high temperatures.

SEM Scanning electron microscopy, used for obtaining high magnification images often in combination with chemical analysis (eg EDS).

Separators Kiln furniture used to separate wares in the kiln.

Sgraffito A style of decoration where a pot is decorated with a slip, and the design is incised through the slip layer to show the contrasting colour of the clay beneath.

Slab building A method of hand-building pottery by assembling slabs of clay.

Slip A suspension of fine particles of clay and other minerals in water, often applied to the surface of the pot as decoration in red, black or white colours, but also used in slip casting.

Slip casting Used for making consistent but complex shapes, such as sanitary ware, by pouring a slip into an absorbent plaster mould.

Stackers Kiln furniture supports used to facilitate stacking ware in the kiln.

Stokehole The accessible opening to a kiln, where fuel is replenished.

Stoneware Pottery fired to a high temperature, in excess of about 1150°C, so that it vitrifies and is more impermeable than earthenware.

Temper Non-plastic material, like shell, ground-up rock, sand and dung, added to clay to modify its properties.

Thin section A slice of pottery, ground very thin so that light can pass through it, used for petrography.

Tin-glaze A lead glaze with tin oxide added to create a consistent, opaque, white background for painted decoration on fine earthenware. The addition of other minerals can create a different colour, eg cobalt will produce a blue tin-glaze.

Tin-glazed earthenware Earthenware pottery with a tin-glaze; also referred to loosely as tin-glazed (eg from the Low Countries), maiolica (Italy) and faience (France).

Transfer printing An 18th-century development, using applied printed patterns for decorating pottery.

Trivet Kiln furniture with three sides or prongs, often used to separate glazed ware during firing.

Turntable A manually operated rotating platform used to assist pottery-making, or decoration, processes.

Updraught kiln A kiln where the hot gases are drawn up through the ware chamber.

Ware chamber The part of a kiln where the pots are placed for firing.

Waster A pot damaged and discarded during production, eg because of underfiring, overfiring or breakage.

Weathering Leaving clay exposed to the elements so that it breaks up and is easier to use.

Wheel-throwing Forming vessels with the aid of a rapidly rotating platform, either manually or mechanically powered.

XP Abbreviation for crossed polars, when using both polarising filters in optical petrography.

6 References

Baker, D 1991 *Potworks: The Industrial Architecture of the Staffordshire Potteries.* London: Royal Commission on the Historical Monuments of England

Barclay, K 2001 *Scientific Analysis of Archaeological Ceramics: A Handbook of Resources.* Oxford: Oxbow

Barker, D and Goodwin, J 2006 'Case study 3: The Beswick pottery, Barford Street, Stoke-on-Trent' *in* English Heritage (ed) *Science for Historic Industries. Guidelines for the Investigation of 17th- to 19th-Century Industries.* Swindon: English Heritage, 8

Barley, M 1964 'The medieval borough of Torksey: Excavations 1960–2'. *Antiq J* **44**, 164–87

Barley, M 1981 'The medieval borough of Torksey: Excavations 1963–8'. *Antiq J* **61**, 264–91

Bates, S 2003a 'Excavations at Heath Farm, Postwick, 1995–6 (Site 31108)' *in* Bates, S and Lyons, A (eds) *The Excavation of Romano-British Pottery Kilns at Ellingham, Postwick and Two Mile Bottom, Norfolk, 1996–7* (East Anglian Arch Occ Papers **13**). Dereham: Norfolk Museums and Archaeology Service, 28–56

Bates, S 2003b 'Excavations at Two Mile Bottom, Thetford, 1995–6 (Site 5738)' *in* Bates, S and Lyons, A (eds) *The Excavation of Romano-British Pottery Kilns at Ellingham, Postwick and Two Mile Bottom, Norfolk, 1996–7* (East Anglian Arch Occ Papers **13**). Dereham: Norfolk Museums and Archaeology Service, 57–95

Bates, S and Lyons, A L 2003 *The Excavation of Romano-British Pottery Kilns at Ellingham, Postwick and Two Mile Bottom, Norfolk, 1996–7* (East Anglian Arch Occ Papers 13). Dereham: Norfolk Museums and Archaeology Service

Best, J and Woodward, A 2012 'Late Bronze Age pottery production site and settlement at Foster's Field, Tinney's Lane, Sherborne'. *Proc Prehist Soc* **78**, 207–61

Best, J, Woodward, A and Tyler, K 2013 *Late Bronze Age Pottery Production; Evidence from a 12th to 11th Century BC Settlement at Tinney's Lane, Sherborne, Dorset* (Dorset Natr Hist Archaeol Soc Monogr Ser **21**). Dorchester: Dorset County Museum

Bowman, S 1990 *Radiocarbon Dating.* British Museum Publications, London

Branigan, K and Foster, P 1995 *Barra: Archaeological Research on Tangaval.* Sheffield: Sheffield Academic Press

Brown, D, 2011 *Archaeological Archives. A Guide to Best Practice in Creation, Compilation, Transfer and Curation.* Archaeological Archive Forum, http://www.archaeologyuk.org/archives/

Bulmer, M 1980 'The finds, pre-Roman to Saxon-Norman' *in* McPeake, J C, Bulmer, M and Rutter, J A (eds), 'Excavations in the garden of No 1 Abbey Green, Chester, 1975–77: Interim report'. *J Chester Archaeol Soc* **63**, 14–37

CIfA 2008a *Standard and Guidance for Excavation.* Reading: Chartered Institute for Archaeologists

CIfA 2008b *Standard and Guidance for the Archaeological Investigation of Standing Buildings or Structures.* Reading: Chartered Institute for Archaeologists

CIfA 2008c *Standard and Guidance for an Archaeological Watching Brief.* Reading: Chartered Institute for Archaeologists

CIfA 2008d *Standard and Guidance for the Collection, Documentation, Conservation and Research of Archaeological Materials.* Reading: Chartered Institute for Archaeologists

CIfA 2009 *Standard and Guidance for Archaeological Field Evaluation.* Reading: Chartered Institute for Archaeologists

CIfA 2012 *Standard and Guidance for Desk-Based Assessment.* Reading: Chartered Institute for Archaeologists

CIfA 2014 *Membership Regulations.* Reading: Chartered Institute for Archaeologists

Cotter, J 2008 'Medieval London-type ware kilns discovered at Woolwich'. *Med Pottery Res Group News* **61**, 3–5

Courty M A and Roux V 1995 'Identification of wheel throwing on the basis of ceramic surface features and microfabrics'. *J Arch Sci* **22**, 17–50

Cuddon, A 1827 *A Representation of the Manufacturing of Earthenware: With Twenty-One Highly Finished Copperplate Engravings, and a Short Explanation of Each, Shewing the Whole Process of the Pottery*. London: Ambrose Cuddon

Cumberpatch, C, Robert, I, Alldritt, D, Batt, C, Gaunt, G, Greenwood, D, Hudson, J, Hughes, M, Ixer, R, Meadows, J, Weston, P and Young, J 2013 'A Stamford ware pottery kiln in Pontefract: A geographical enigma and a dating dilemma'. *Med Arch* **57**, 111–50

Darling, M 1994 *Guidelines for the Archiving of Roman Pottery*. London: Study Group for Roman Pottery

Dawson, A 1997 'The growth of the Staffordshire ceramic industry' *in* Freestone, I and Gaimster, D (eds) *Pottery in the Making. World Ceramic Traditions*. London: British Museum Press, 200–5

Dawson, D and Kent, O 1999 'Reduction fired low-temperature ceramics'. *Post-Med Arch* **33**, 164–78

Dawson, D and Kent, O 2008 'The development of the bottle kiln in pottery manufacture in Britain'. *Post-Med Arch* **42**, 201–26

Dawson, D and Kent, O 2012 *The Pottery House in the Park, Dunster; A Rare Survival of an 18th-Century Pottery Kiln*. Dulverton: Exmoor National Park Authority

Dawson, G 1971 'Two tin-glazed kilns at Montague Close, Southwark: Part 1, excavation; Part 2, preliminary report on the pottery'. *London Arch* **1**, 228–31 and 250–51

Day, P M, Kiriatzi, E, Tsolakidou, A and Kilikoglou, V 1999 'Group therapy in Crete: A comparison between analysis by NAA and thin section petrography'. *J Arch Sci* **26**, 1025–36

Divers, D and Jarrett, C 2008 'Chapter 5: Delftware production at Southwark Cathedral' *in* Divers, D, Mayo, C, Cohen, N and Jarrett, C A *New Millennium at Southwark Cathedral: Investigations into the First Two Thousand Years* (Pre-Construct Archaeol Monogr **8**). Durham: Pre-Construct Archaeology Ltd, 101–24

Drury, P 1981 'The production of brick and tile in medieval England' *in* Crossley, D (ed) *Medieval Industry* (CBA Res Rep **40**). London: Council for British Archaeology, 126–42

Duller, G 2008 *Luminescence Dating. Guidelines on Using Luminescence Dating in Archaeology*. Swindon: English Heritage

Dunning, G 1959 'IV. Pottery of the late Anglo-Saxon period on England' *in* Dunning, G, Hurst, J, Myres, J and Tischler, F 'Anglo-Saxon Pottery: A Symposium', *Med Arch* **3**, 1–78

English Heritage 2006a *Management of Research Projects in the Historic Environment. The MoRPHE Project Managers' Guide*. Swindon: English Heritage

English Heritage 2006b *Science for Historic Industries. Guidelines for the Investigation of 17th- to 19th-Century Industries*. Swindon: English Heritage

English Heritage 2006c *Archaeomagnetic Dating. Guidelines on Producing and Interpreting Archaeomagnetic Dates*. Swindon: English Heritage.

English Heritage 2006d *Understanding Historic Buildings. A Guide to Good Recording Practice*. Swindon: English Heritage

English Heritage 2008a *Geophysical Survey in Archaeological Field Evaluation*. Swindon: English Heritage

English Heritage 2008b *Investigative Conservation. Guidelines on How the Detailed Examination of Artefacts from Archaeological Sites can Shed Light on their Manufacture and Use*. Swindon: English Heritage

English Heritage 2011a *Environmental Archaeology. A Guide to the Theory and Practice of Methods, from Sampling and Recovery to Post-Excavation*, 2 edn. Swindon: English Heritage

English Heritage 2011b *Designation Listing Selection Guide. Industrial Structures*. Swindon: English Heritage

Evans, C, Jenks, W and White, R 1999 'Romano-British kilns at Meole Brace (Pulley), Shropshire'. *Trans Shropshire Arch Soc* **74**, 1–27

Evans, C J, Jones, L and Eliis, P 2000 *Severn Valley Ware Production at Newland Hopfield. Excavation of a Romano-British Kiln Site at North End Farm, Great Malvern, Worcestershire in 1992 and 1994* (BAR Brit Ser **313**). Oxford: Archaeopress

Gaimster, D 1997a 'Regional decorative traditions in English post-medieval slipware' *in* Freestone, I and Gaimster, D (eds) *Pottery in the Making. World Ceramic Traditions*. London: British Museum Press, 128–33

Gaimster, D 1997b 'Stoneware production in medieval and early modern Germany' *in* Freestone, I and Gaimster, D (eds) *Pottery in the Making. World Ceramic Traditions*. London: British Museum Press, 122–7

Gibson, A and Woods, A 1997 *Prehistoric Pottery for the Archaeologist*. Leicester: Leicester University Press

Gosselain, O P 1999 'In pots we trust: The processing of clay and symbols in Sub-Saharan Africa'. *J Material Culture* **4**, 205–30

Gould, S 2008 *Understanding Historic Buildings: Policy and Guidance for Local Planning Authorities*. Swindon: English Heritage

Green, C M 1999 *John Dwight's Fulham Pottery: Excavations 1971–79* (English Heritage Arch Rep **6**). Swindon: English Heritage

Greenwood, D, Batt, C, Bronk Ramsey, C, Cook, G, Meadows, J and Roberts, I 2010 *Simpson's Malt, Pontefract, West Yorkshire: Scientific Dating of a Pottery Kiln* (English Heritage Res Dept Rep Ser **60–2010**). Swindon: English Heritage

Gregory, R A 2004 'Rediscovering the Denaby pottery: Archaeological investigations at Denaby Main, Conisbrough, South Yorkshire'. *Post-Med Arch* **38**, 133–80

Haggarty, G, Hall, D and Jones, R 2011 'Sourcing Scottish medieval ceramics: The use and success of chemical analysis'. *Proc Soc Antiq Scot* **141**, 249–67

Haith, C 1997 'Pottery in early Anglo-Saxon England' *in* Freestone, I and Gaimster, D (eds) *Pottery in the Making. World Ceramic Traditions*. London: British Museum Press, 146–51

Hamilton, S 2002 'Between ritual and routine: Interpreting British prehistoric pottery production and distribution' *in* Woodward, A and Hill, J D (eds) *Prehistoric Britain: The Ceramic Basis*. Oxford: Oxbow Books, 38–53

Hill, J D 2002 'Just about the potter's wheel? Using, making and depositing middle and later Iron Age pots in East Anglia' *in* Woodward, A and Hill, J D (eds) *Prehistoric Britain: The Ceramic Basis*. Oxford: Oxbow Books, 143–60

Hull, M 1963 *The Roman Potters' Kilns of Colchester*. London: Society of Antiquaries

Hurst, J D, 1994 'A medieval ceramic production site and other medieval sites in the parish of Hanley Castle; results of fieldwork in 1987–1992'. *Trans Worcestershire Archaeol Soc* **3** ser **14**, 115–28

Hurst, D and Freestone, I C 1996 'Lead glazing technique from a medieval kiln site at Hanley Swan, Worcestershire'. *Med Ceramics* **20**, 13–18

Irving, A 2011 *A Research Framework for Post-Roman Ceramic Studies in Britain* (MPRG Occ Paper **6**). London: Medieval Pottery Research Group

Ladle, L and Woodward, A 2009 *Excavations at Bestwall Quarry, Wareham, 1992–2005: The Prehistoric Landscape* (Dorset Natr Hist Archaeol Soc Monogr Ser **18**). Dorchester: Dorset Natural History and Archaeological Society

Le Patourel, H E J 1968 'Documentary evidence and the medieval pottery industry'. *Med Arch* **12**, 104–26

Mayes, P and Scott, K 1984 *Pottery Kilns at Chilvers Coton, Nuneaton*. London: Society for Medieval Archaeology

McCarthy, M R and Brooks, C M 1988 *Medieval Pottery in Britain AD 900–1600*. Leicester: Leicester University Press

Middleton, A 1997 'Tiles in Roman Britain' *in* Freestone, I and Gaimster, D (eds) *Pottery in the Making. World Ceramic Traditions*. London: British Museum Press, 158–63

Miles, P, Young, J and Wacher, J 1989 *A Late Saxon Kiln Site at Silver Street, Lincoln*. Lincoln: City of Lincoln Archaeology Unit

Moorhouse, S 1981 'The medieval pottery industry and its markets' *in* Crossley, D (ed) *Medieval Industry* (CBA Res Rep **40**). York: Council for British Archaeology, 96–125

Moorhouse, S and Roberts, I 1992 *Wrenthorpe Potteries. Excavations of 16th- and 17th-Century Potting Tenements near Wakefield, 1983-86* (Yorkshire Arch **2**). Leeds: West Yorkshire Archaeology Service

Mountford, A, Gee, J and Simpson G, 1968 'Excavation of an early Neronian pottery kiln and workshop at Trent Vale, Stoke-on-Trent'. *Staffordshire J Field Studies* **8**, 19–38

MPRG 2001 *Minimum Standards for the Processing, Recording and Analysis and Publication of Post-Roman Ceramics* (MPRG Occ Paper **2**). London: Medieval Pottery Research Group

Musty, J 1974 'Medieval pottery kilns' *in* Evison, V, Hodges, H and Hurst, J (eds) *Medieval Pottery from Excavations: Studies Presented to Gerald Clough Dunning*. London: John Baker, 49–65

Newell, R W 1995 'Some notes on "splashed glazes"'. *Med Ceramics* **19**, 77–88

NPPF 2012 *National Planning and Policy Framework*. London: Department for Communities and Local Government

Orton, C and Hughes, M 2013 *Pottery in Archaeology* (Cambridge Manuals in Archaeology). Cambridge: Cambridge University Press

Oxford Archaeology North 2012 *Grimshaw Pottery, Blackburn, Lancashire: Final Archive Report*. Lancaster: Oxford Archaeology North, http://archaeologydataservice.ac.uk/archiveDS/archiveDownload?t=arch-815-1/dissemination/pdf/oxfordar2-150218_1.pdf

Palmer, M, Nevell, M and Sissons, M 2012 *Industrial Archaeology: A Handbook* (CBA Practical Handbook **21**). York: Council for British Archaeology

Paynter, S 2000 *Analysis of 17th-Century Delftware Pottery Sherds from London* (Ancient Monuments Lab Rep **56/2000**). Swindon: English Heritage

Paynter, S, Rollo, L and McSloy, E, 2009 'Made in the Nene Valley? Identifying the origins of mortaria using ICP analysis'. *J Arch Sci* **36**, 1390–9

PCRG 2011 *The Study of Later Prehistoric Pottery: General Policies and Guidelines for Analysis and Publications* (MPRG Occ Paper **1** and **2**, 3 rev edn). London: Medieval Pottery Research Group

Peacock, D P S 1968 'A petrological study of certain Iron Age pottery from Western England'. *Proc Prehist Soc* **34**, 414–27

Peacock, D P S 1982 *Pottery in the Roman World: An Ethnoarchaeological Approach.* London: Longman

Pearce, J 1984 'Getting a handle on medieval pottery'. *London Arch* **5**, 17–23

Pearson, T 2011 *Introduction to Heritage Assets, Roman and Medieval Pottery and Tile Production.* Swindon: English Heritage

Perrin, R 2011 *A Research Strategy and Updated Agenda for the Study of Roman Pottery in Britain* (SGRP Occ Paper **1**). London: Study Group for Roman Pottery

Perrin, K, Brown, D H, Lange, G, Bibby, D, Carlsson, A, Degraeve, A, Kuna, M, Larsson, Y, Pálsdóttir, S U, Stoll-Tucker, B, Dunning, C, Rogalla von Bieberstein, A, 2014 *A Standard and Guide to Best Practice for Archaeological Archiving in Europe* (EAC Guidelines **1**). Namur: Europae Archaeologia Consilium (EAC) http://archaeologydataservice.ac.uk/arches/Wiki.jsp

Perry, G J 2013 'United in death: The pre burial origins of Anglo-Saxon cremation urns'. Unpublished PhD thesis, Univ Sheffield

Perry, G J (in prep) 'Pottery production in Anglo-Scandinavian Torksey (Lincolnshire): Reconstructing and contextualising the chaîne opératoire'. *Med Arch*

Pre-Construct Archaeology Ltd 2014 *Land East of Moorfield Road and South of A505, Duxford, Cambridgeshire: Archaeological Excavation* (PCA Rep **R11661**). Stapleford: Pre-Construct Archaeology Ltd

Quinn, P 2013 *Ceramic Petrography: The Interpretation of Archaeological Pottery and Related Artefacts in Thin Section.* Oxford: Archaeopress

Roberts, I and Cumberpatch, C 2009 'A Stamford ware pottery kiln in Pontefract'. *Med Arch* **53**, 371–6

Roberts, P 1997 'Mass-production of Roman finewares' *in* Freestone, I and Gaimster, D (eds) *Pottery in the Making. World Ceramic Traditions.* London: British Museum Press, 188–93

Rye, O 1981 *Pottery Technology: Principles and Reconstruction* (Manuals Arch **4**). Washington: Taraxacum

Seeley, F and Drummond-Murray, J 2005 *Roman Pottery Production in the Walbrook Valley. Excavations at 20–28 Moorgate, City of London, 1998–2000* (MoLAS Monogr **25**). London: Museum of London Archaeology Service

Sillar, B 2000 *Shaping Culture: Making Pots and Constructing Households. An Ethnoarchaeological Study of Pottery Production, Trade and Use in the Andes* (BAR Int Ser **883**). Oxford: Archaeopress

Simco, A 1998 *The Clay Industries* (English Heritage Monuments Protection Programme Step 1 Report). Swindon: English Heritage

Simco, A 2000 *The Clay Industries* (English Heritage Monuments Protection Programme Step 2 Shortlist). Swindon: English Heritage

Stocker, D 2006 *England's Landscape: The East Midlands.* London: Collins

Swan, V 1984 *The Pottery Kilns of Roman Britain* (RCHME Suppl Ser **5**). London: Her Majesty's Stationary Office

The Prince's Regeneration Trust 2012 *Middleport Pottery, Burslem, Stoke on Trent. Conservation Management Plan.* London: The Prince's Regeneration Trust

Timby, J 1988 'The Middle Saxon pottery' in Andrews, P (ed) *The Coins and Pottery from Hamwic.* Southampton: Southampton City Museums, 73–122

Tomber, R and Dore, J 1998 *The National Roman Fabric Reference Collection. A Handbook* (MoLAS Monogr **2**). London: Museum of London Archaeology Service

Tyler, K, Betts, I and Stephenson, R 2008 *London's Delftware Industry: The Tin-Glazed Pottery Industries of Southwark and Lambeth* (MoLA Monogr 40). London: Museum of London Archaeology

Varndell, G and Freestone, I 1997 'Early prehistoric pottery in Britain' *in* Freestone, I and Gaimster, D (eds) *Pottery in the Making. World Ceramic Traditions.* London: British Museum Press, 32–7

Vince, A 1993 'Forms, functions and manufacturing techniques of late ninth- and tenth-century wheelthrown pottery in England and their origins' *in* Piton, D (ed) *La céramique du 5ème au 10ème siècle dans l'Europa du Nord-Ouest: travaux du Groupe de Recherches et d'Etudes sur la Céramique dans le Nord, Pas-de-Calais (Actes du colloque d'Outreau 10–12 Avril 1992)* (Hors-série de Nord-Ouest Archéologie). Berck-sur-Mer: CRADC, 151–64

Watkinson, D and Neal, V 2001 *First Aid for Finds: Practical Guide for Archaeologists*, 3 edn. London: Rescue/UK United Kingdom Institute for Conservation Archaeology Section

Whitbread, I K 1995 *Greek Transport Amphorae: A Petrological and Archaeological Study* (Fitch Lab Occ Papers **4**). Oxford: Oxbow Books

White, H 2012 'The problem of provenancing English post-medieval slipwares: a chemical and petrographic approach'. *Post-Med Arch* **46/1**, 56–69

Wild, J P 1973 'A fourth-century potter's workshop and kilns at Stibbington, Peterborough' *in* Detsicas, A (ed) *Current Research in Romano-British Coarse Pottery* (CBA Res Rep **10**). York: Council for British Archaeology, 135–8

Wilson, M A, Hamilton, A, Ince, C, Carter, M A, Hall, C 2012 'Rehydroxylation (RHX) dating of archaeological pottery'. *Proc Royal Soc A* **468**, 3476–93

Woodward, A 2002 'Inclusions, impressions and interpretation' *in* Woodward, A and Hill, J D (eds) *Prehistoric Britain: The Ceramic Basis*. Oxford: Oxbow Books, 106–18

Young, C 1971 'A pottery mould fragment from Littlemore, Oxon'. *Britannia* **2**, 238–40

Acknowledgements

These guidelines were written and compiled by Harriet White, Sarah Paynter and Duncan Brown with contributions by Joanne Best, Chris Cumberpatch, David Dawson, Peter Ellis, Jane Evans, Laurence Jones, Oliver Kent, Gareth Perry, The Prince's Regeneration Trust, Ian Roberts, Kerry Tyler and Ann Woodward. The layout was arranged by Vince Griffin and the text edited by Eva Fairnell.

We are indebted to the following organisations and individuals for providing illustrations: David Dawson, Oliver Kent, Gareth Perry, Bill Sillar, Ian Roberts, Archaeological Services WYAS, The Prince's Regeneration Trust, Jane Evans, John Cotter and Oxford Archaeology, Fiona Seeley, Andy Chopping and Museum of London Archaeology, Thames Valley Archaeological Services, Bristol Museums, Galleries and Archives, the Museum of Barnstaple and North Devon, Somerset Heritage Service, the Trustees of the British Museum, Chard Museum, Bristol and Region Archaeological Services, North Lincoln Museum, The Collection Museum, the Historic England Archive, the Torksey Viking Project and Southampton City Council Arts and Heritage.

We would like to thank all those who responded to consultation with improvements to the original text, including: Gareth Perry, Jonathan Last, Chris Cumberpatch, Jim Williams, Andy Hammon, David Dungworth, Margaret Ward, Sue Stallibrass, Ben Jervis, John Cotter, Luke Barber, Peter Marshall, David Dawson, Oliver Kent, Paul Booth, Shane Gould, Angela Middleton, Karla Graham, Paul Linford, Derek Hurst, Fiona Seeley, Ann Woodward, Anne Jenner, Paul Gardner, Edward Holland, Tim Howard, and the SGRP, MPRG, PCRG and CIfA.

This page is left blank intentionally

We are the public body that looks after England's historic environment. We champion historic places, helping people understand, value and care for them.

Please contact
guidance@HistoricEngland.org.uk
with any questions about this document.

HistoricEngland.org.uk

If you would like this document in a different format, please contact our customer services department on:

Tel: 0370 333 0607
Fax: 01793 414926
Textphone: 0800 015 0174
Email: customers@HistoricEngland.org.uk

HEAG019
Publication date: v1.0 October 2015
Design: Historic England

Printed in Dunstable, United Kingdom